Thimbleberries®

Collection of Classic Quilts

by Lynette Jensen

An inspiring gallery of 26 classic quilts featuring
the best of Thimbleberries® enduring quilt
patterns updated with today's newest colors.

LANDAUER BOOKS

This book was designed, produced, and published by Landauer Books
A division of Landauer Corporation
3100 NW 101st Street, Urbandale, IA 50322

President: Jeramy Lanigan Landauer
Operations Director: Kitty Jacobson
Editor-in-Chief: Becky Johnston
Art Director: Laurel Albright
Creative Director: Lynette Jensen
Photographers: Craig Anderson and Dennis Kennedy
Photostyling: Lynette Jensen and Margaret Sindelar
Technical Writer: Sue Bahr
Graphic Technician: DeWayne Studer
Technical Illustrators: Lisa Kirchoff, Linda Bender, and Marcia Cameron

We also wish to thank the support staff of the Thimbleberries® Design Studio:
Sherry Husske, Virginia Brodd, Renae Ashwill, Ardelle Paulson, Kathy Lobeck, Carla Plowman,
Julie Jergens, Pearl Baysinger, Tracy Schrantz, Leone Rusch, Julie Borg, Clarine Howe and Ellen Carter.

ISBN13: 978-1-890621-88-9
ISBN10:   1-890621-88-9

Printed in China 10 9 8 7 6 5 4 3

Library of Congress Cataloging-in-Publication Data available on request.

FOREWORD

Twenty-eight years ago,

I fell in love with antique quilts. I loved their color, design, geometry and what quilts represent—comfort, home, and family—so I decided to create my own. After learning how to quilt, one thing led to another and soon I was teaching the art of quilt-making, which ultimately led to designing quilt patterns.

The coordination of prints, colors, and quilt patterns created a distinctive look. I discovered that by designing my own line of coordinating prints, solids, and plaids, I could get exactly what I needed for my growing collection of pieced patchwork. A licensing agreement with RJR Fabrics has resulted in an expansive line of fabrics anchored by my signature Paintbox Collection™. Thimbleberries® fabrics are featured in about 2,500 independent quilt shops and nearly 850 of these shops host a Thimbleberries® Quilt Club that meets regularly.

One of the reasons Thimbleberries® has been so well-received is that I make it easy for quilters to enjoy the wonderful heritage craft of quilt-making. Today's quilters have limited time. I carved my niche by showing quilters what to do with the fabrics without spending a lifetime creating a quilt. In 25 years of teaching, I've also developed a system of quilt-making that uses clear and simple instructions to help even first-time quilters build confidence and skills.

In the pages of this book, you'll find a collection of 26 classic quilts featuring the best of Thimbleberries®. It is my hope that these enduring quilt patterns will help you transform your home into a welcoming place that will hug you back!

My Best,

Lynette Jensen

Table of Contents

INTRODUCTION

Lynette Jensen

Lynette Jensen is an acclaimed designer, best-selling author, and renowned educator who has earned success creating the fabric of life—and a comfortable lifestyle—for millions of Thimbleberries® fans worldwide.

Recognized as a leading fabric designer in the independent quilt industry, Lynette is the best-selling author of seven books for Landauer Corporation, three books for Rodale Press, two books for C & T Publishing, and more than 100 self-published Thimbleberries® books and patterns with nearly a million copies sold.

In today's hectic, hurried, high-tech world, more and more people continue to look toward the centuries' old craft of quilting as a way to relax while creating something wonderful to enhance their homes.

Showing people how to surround themselves with familiar pieces from the past to make their homes warm and inviting is Lynette Jensen's specialty.

For the past 14 years Lynette has been at the forefront of the home arts as president of her highly visible company, Thimbleberries®, which offers consumers coordinating fabric print collections and the ability to put them together in a clear, graphic sense to create a quality hand-crafted product.

Lynette has built a successful business by offering these customers of

over 2,500 independent quilt and craft shops something they never could do before: enjoy the fruits of their labor—without laboring too much! Through her quilt designs, Lynette has helped millions of consumers easily recreate in their homes a lifestyle similar to her own, one she holds dear.

Designing from her traditional point of view, Lynette introduces six to eight collections a year in all-cotton and cotton flannel with between 24 and 75 skus per collection, with an average of eight prints in three colorways.

Some of Lynette's designs are direct reproductions, some are a combination of inspirations, and generally the colorways are traditional.

Her personal sense of style—and lifestyle—is decidedly casual, easy to live with, comfortable and practical, not fussy or ostentatious.
Lynette has a sense of who she is and surrounds herself and family with antiques and home accessories such as old pottery pieces that, like her quilts, evoke honest warmth and ease.

Lynette's ultimate goal is to build confidence in other people to surround themselves with favorite furnishings that are easily coordinated, comfortable and cozy. With so many people who identify with the way Lynette lives and who try to emulate her approachable—and doable lifestyle, Thimbleberries® has almost worldwide appeal.

Themes for decorating can range from traditional to contemporary, but the key is keeping it casual. Whether you fill your home with priceless antiques or garage-sale finds, the finished feeling should be one of welcoming comfort.

And regardless of size, from cottage to castle, by following Lynette Jensen's lead, almost anyone can create a cozy, quilt-filled place called home.

Through her many books Lynette shares her lifestyle secrets for decorating, entertaining, creating projects and quilting inspirations through a personal tour of her home and gardens. Lynette shows how to mix and match colors, blend decorating styles, and highlight favorite family pieces using a simple planning process that takes the reader from basic to beautiful in a matter of minutes.

$\mathcal{T}$*he photographs on these two pages* are a "classic"
example of how Lynette's decorating can move through the seasons. Her
black-and-cream buffalo check sofas anchor a living room through four
seasons of decorating from spring and summer to autumn and Christmas
shown here. Lynette transitions the seasons with accessories that make one
feel truly at home.

Whether decorating, gardening, entertaining, cooking or crafting, Lynette, who lives with her husband Neil in a lovingly restored two-story Colonial home in a small town in Minnesota, does it well with warmth and humor.

Lynette's close family includes a grown son, Matthew, a daughter, Kerry, and son-in-law Trevor, and an extended family of relatives and friends who all love nothing better than to congregate there for a terrific reason: Lynette has created a comfortable environment where everyone feels at home. It's what she does best.

OVERVIEW

Thimbleberries®

Lynette Jensen feels strongly that a well-designed quilt should stand the test of time and be as useful as it is attractive. These are just a few of the criteria that Lynette follows for each of the hundreds of Thimbleberries® quilts that she has designed over the years.

For every quilt that Lynette designs, there is much more than just what meets the eye. On the following pages, discover how the color palette, the fabrics, the style, the blocks, the appliqué, the backing, and the quilting all work together to create the distinctive look and timeless comfort of a classic Thimbleberries® quilt.

Old-fashioned country scrap quilts have heavily influenced Lynette Jensen's preferences in fabric design. Lynette enjoys the challenge of blending a large number of fabrics into a pleasing collection featuring the following elements:

- PRINTED PLAINS are tone-on-tone color combinations with subtle, all over random prints treated as a solid color in a quilt.

- SMALL BLENDER PRINTS are great blenders, offering color, design, and texture without a lot of differences in color values.

- LARGE-SCALE PRINTS are best used effectively as outside borders and large patches and alternating, unpieced blocks—usually no more than one per quilt.

- WOVEN PLAIDS & CHECKS add a bit of geometry and a rest for the eye between the Small Blenders and the Large-Scale Prints. They should be used sparingly because the bold images or strong color definition can sometimes interfere with and distract from the pieced design.

NOTE: *The fabrics shown here are some of Lynette's all-time favorites and may or may not be currently available. However, the unique feature of Thimbleberries® is that the fabrics can easily be mixed and matched because they blend from group to group.*

Printed PLAINS

Small Blender PRINTS

Large Scale PRINTS

Woven PLAIDS & CHECKS

Printed GEOMETRICS

Lynette Jensen often refers to her quilt designs as "prairie patchwork" with the focus on straight lines, simple bold shapes, and pattern repeats. The Prairie Pines quilt shown below is a classic example of the enduring quality of Thimbleberries®—it is the first design Lynette offered as a pattern more than a decade ago and remains firmly established in the Thimbleberries® line of patterns and books today.

When designing a quilt for Thimbleberries®, Lynette also places a great deal of emphasis on traditional quilt patterns and symmetry, in addition to the straight lines, simple bold shapes, and repetition of pattern.

Holiday Bouquet, shown opposite, is a classic example of the best of Thimbleberries®. Each floral block is bordered by a row of Flying Geese— a traditional quilt pattern. The four blocks and the border appliqués are clearly mirror images for symmetry and provide balanced repetition of pattern.(To make Holiday Bouquet, turn to page 44 for complete instructions and full-size patterns for the quilt.)

Patterns inspired by traditional quilt blocks are classic elements in the quilts that Lynette Jensen designs for Thimbleberries®. Quilt blocks date back to the early American colonists who could not afford to make wholecloth quilts which required relatively large pieces of fabric. Out of thrift and necessity, the pioneer settlers made use of every scrap of fabric and cleverly discovered how to combine these scraps into individual blocks that could be set aside until there were enough completed blocks to assemble into a whole quilt.

A collection of blocks could be quickly assembled into a quilt at a quilting bee, and as a result, block patterns became a tradition in their own right. The pioneer women often named the pieced patchwork blocks after ordinary household objects or their surroundings, such as a log cabin, a bear's paw, and flying geese.

Log Cabin is an all-time favorite block since the mid-1800s. Successively longer strips of fabric are sewn clockwise around a center square as if building a cabin of logs. The blocks are assembled into a multitude of arrangements—such as Barn Raising, Straight Furrows, Streak of Lightning, Medallion, and Sunshine and Shadow. (To make the Garden Scape Quilt, please turn to page 178.)

Nine-Patch is the result of the frugal use of fabrics when fabric was scarce in Colonial days. Patch blocks were often taught to young girls as they pieced their first quilts, often at the ages of 10 or 11. The patch block was often used as the basis for piecing utilitarian quilts. (To make the Daisy Days Nine-Patch Quilt, please turn to page 130.)

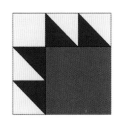

Bear's Paw is a unique combination of squares and half-square triangles that can be set into a variety of pleasing arrangements. The block was thought to be a way for pioneer women to connect with the adventure of the New Frontier from the relative snug safety of their homes. (To make the Pine Star Runner, please turn to page 82).

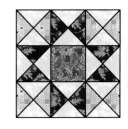

Pinwheel blocks were inspired by a familiar sight on the American prairie landscape—the windmill. The pinwheel was considered a bit more challenging for a Colonial quilter because the points of each pinwheel required precise hand-piecing. (To make the Party Pinwheels Quilt, please turn to page 190.)

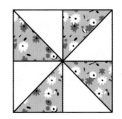

Stars of all shapes and sizes may have been inspired by the early settlers fascination with the skies as they traveled through the wilderness, often at night to avoid the heat of the day. The star block pattern is frequently used in sampler quilts in an endless variety of color combinations. (To make the September Stars Quilt, please turn to page 202.)

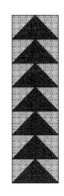

Flying Geese features blocks that begin with a large floral motif bordered by a row of Flying Geese. Likely inspired by the sight and sound of large honking geese flying overhead, the women of the frontier and early settlements incorporated what they saw in their daily lives into useful objects such as quilts and table runners. (To make the Holiday Bouquet Quilt, please turn to page 44.)

Lynette Jensen uses appliqué effectively in many of the quilts she designs for Thimbleberries®. As much a part of quilt-making as is piecing, appliqué is simply the art of cutting out pieces of fabric to apply to the surface of another fabric. By combining appliqué with patchwork, Lynette creates added dimension and interest to quilts. Her designs for appliqué range from simple bold shapes and repeated center motifs for blocks to an appealing array of twining vines, berries, and blossoms for borders. The result is a charming blend of blocks and borders with soft touches of country color for a unique style reminiscent of America's more tranquil past.

Harvest Apple

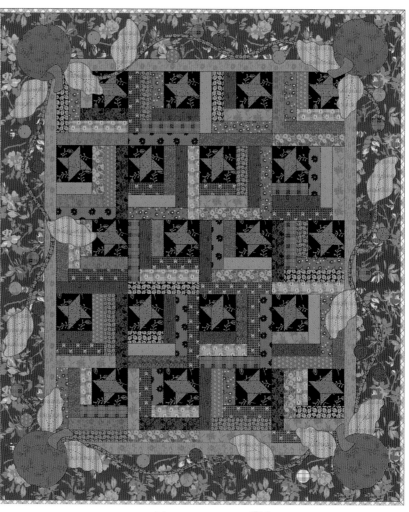

Midnight Sky

Sunporch Basket

Lynette Jensen considers the backing of any Thimbleberries® quilt to be just as important to the overall design as is the pieced patchwork top. She often uses large-scale prints or pieces coordinating fabrics together to create an interesting quilt back. Using really large pieces of fabric (perhaps three different prints that are the same length as the quilt) or a large piece of fabric that is bordered by compatible prints, keeps the number of seams to a minimum, which speeds up the quilting process. Carefully selected fabrics for a well-constructed backing not only complement a finished quilt, they make it more useful as a reversible accent as shown opposite.

Twin
72 x 90-inches

5-1/4 yards
Cut 2, 2-5/8 yard lengths

Crib
45 x 60-inches

2-3/4 yards
Cut 2, 1-3/8 yard lengths

Double/Full
81 x 96-inches

7-1/8 yards
Cut 3, 2-3/8 yard lengths

Queen
90 x 108-inches

8 yards
Cut 3, 2-5/8 yard lengths

For Lynette Jensen, choosing a quilting design to complement the finished quilt requires as much attention as the construction of the quilt itself. There are three methods of quilting that work well for a variety of quilts:

* OUTLINE QUILTING follows the outline and accentuates the shape of a pieced or appliquéd block by stitching very close to the seam line or as much as 1/4 inch away from the seam line.

* BACKGROUND QUILTING fills large spaces and puts more emphasis on the quilt patterns by making them stand out from the background. Background quilting can be done in straight lines or in a random pattern.

* DESIGN QUILTING is often a decorative accent in its own right. Popular designs include feathers, wreaths, cables, and swags which work well in open spaces such as large corner blocks or borders.

Crossroads
Outline Quilting

Holiday Bouquet
Background Quilting

Courtyard Garden

Prairie Pines

Design Quilting

Crossroads

Holiday Bouquet

Courtyard Garden

Prairie Pines

33

PREVIEW

Chapters

Lynette Jensen has gathered 26 of her best-selling Thimbleberries® quilt designs into one collection featured on the following pages in three distinct groupings. Ranging in size from small to medium and to large, many of the pieced quilts and table runners are accented with easy appliqué which will appeal to a wide audience of quilters.

The quilts and table runners are grouped by size into three chapters: Seasonal Wonders, Cottage Throws, and Sleeping Beauties. Each chapter includes enduring quilt patterns updated with today's newest colors from Lynette's classic Thimbleberries® fabric collections.

Whether you're a beginner, intermediate, or even a master quilter, you'll find a Thimbleberries® quilt well worth the time and investment it takes to make a keepsake quilt that will pass from generation to generation.

Frosty Lights

In keeping with the
Christmas spirit,
light-hearted piecing and
easy appliqué will add
a bit of whimsy to a
wall-hanging sized just right
for holiday gift giving!

Frosty Lights

Quilt measures 28 inches.

Fabric & Supplies

1/4 yard	**RED PRINT** for triangle blocks
1/4 yard	**TAN PRINT** for triangle blocks
1/4 yard	**GREEN PLAID** for squares
8-1/2-inch square	**BEIGE PRINT** for block background
3/4 yard	**GREEN PRINT** for border
11-inch square	**CREAM** for snowman appliqué (wool, optional)
4-inch square	**BLACK** for hat and button appliqués (wool, optional)
5-inch square	**PLAID** for scarf appliqué (cut on the bias)
1/8 yard	**GREEN CHECK** for light base appliqués
4-inch squares	**ASSORTED FABRICS** (20 squares) for light bulb appliqués
3/8 yard	**RED PRINT** for binding
1 yard	Backing fabric
Quilt batting	32 inches square
3/4 yard	Paper-backed fusible web

#8 Black and gold pearl cotton for appliqué

#5 Gold pearl cotton for light cord

NOTE: read **Getting Started**, page 216, before beginning this project.

Quilt Center

Cutting

From **BEIGE PRINT** cut
- 1— 8-1/2-inch square.

From **RED PRINT** cut
- 4—4-1/2 x 8-1/2-inch rectangles.

From **TAN PRINT** cut
- 8—4-1/2-inch squares.

From **GREEN PLAID** cut
- 4—4-1/2-inch squares.

Piecing

1. Right sides together, position a 4-1/2-inch TAN PRINT square on the corner of a 4-1/2 x 8-1/2-inch RED PRINT rectangle. Draw a diagonal line on the TAN PRINT square and stitch on the line. Trim seam allowance to 1/4 inch; press. Repeat to sew a TAN PRINT square on the opposite side of the RED PRINT rectangle.

Make 4

2. Sew a Step 1 unit to the top and bottom of the 8-1/2-inch BEIGE PRINT square; press.

Make 1

3. Sew a 4-1/2-inch GREEN PLAID square to both ends of the remaining Step 1 units; press. Make 2 units. Sew the units to both side edges of the Step 2 unit; press.

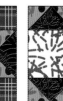

Make 1

Appliquéing the Snowman Block

1. Trace the snowman onto fusible web. Draw a line about 1/4 inch inside the first line.

2. Cut away the fusible web on the inner drawn line.

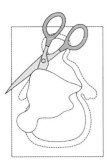 

*Cut out on the
inner drawn line*
(Step 2)

*Cut out on the
outer traced line*
(Step 3)

3. Fuse the snowman shape to the wrong side of the CREAM fabric with a hot, dry iron. Let the fabric cool. Cut out the snowman on the outer drawn line. Remove the paper backing.

4. Paper side up, position the fusible web on the hat, scarf, and button shapes. Trace the shapes, allowing 1/4 inch between each item. Roughly cut around each shape.

5. Place the fusible-web shapes, coated side down, on the wrong side of the fabrics for appliqué. (NOTE: To create a windblown effect for the scarf, place the scarf shape on the bias of the plaid fabric.) Press the fusible web to the fabric with a hot, dry iron. Let the fabric cool. Then cut out the shapes on the tracing lines. Remove the paper backing.

6. Center the snowman shape on the pieced block. Layer the hat, scarf, and buttons on the snowman. Press in place with a hot, dry iron.

7. Using #8 black pearl cotton, buttonhole-stitch the snowman and scarf to the quilt center. Using #8 gold pearl cotton, buttonhole-stitch the hat and buttons to the quilt center. Straight-stitch the eyes, nose, and mouth with #8 black pearl cotton.

Border

NOTE: *The yardage allows for the border strips to be cut on the crosswise grain.*

Cutting

From GREEN PRINT cut
- 3—6-1/2 x 42-inch border strips.

Attaching the Border

1. Measure the quilt from left to right through the center to determine the length of the top and bottom border strips. Cut 2, 6-1/2-inch wide GREEN PRINT strips to this length, sew them to the top and bottom of the quilt, and press the seams toward the border.

2. Measure the quilt from top to bottom through the center, including the border strips just sewn on, to determine the length of the side border strips. Cut 2, 6-1/2-inch wide GREEN PRINT strips to this length, sew them to the sides of the quilt, and press the seams toward the border.

Appliquéing the Lights

1. Position the fusible web, paper side up, on the light bulb and base. Allowing 1/4 inch between shapes, trace each light and base 20 times. Roughly cut out each shape.

2. Place the fusible web shapes, coated side down, on the wrong side of the fabrics for appliqué; press the webbing to the fabric. Let the fabric cool, cut out the shapes, and remove the paper backing.

3. Referring to the quilt illustration, position the lights and bases along the quilt border. Press the shapes in place with a hot, dry iron.

4. Use #8 black pearl cotton to buttonhole-stitch the lights and bases to the border.

NOTE: *Connect the lights with stitched cording after the project is quilted; the thickness of the quilted piece supports the application of the cord and prevents puckering, which could occur on a single layer of fabric.*

Pattern Notes

Appliqué Pieces

The appliqué pieces are reversed images for tracing onto fusible web. When the appliqué is finished, it will appear as it does in the photograph of the finished quilt.

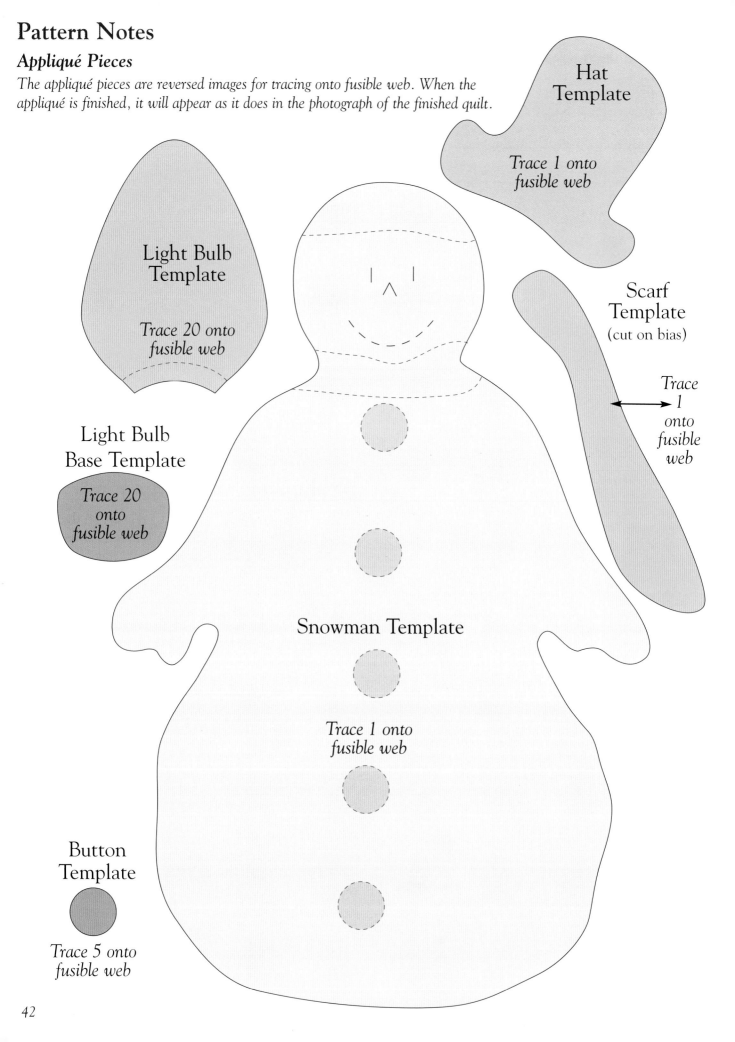

Hat
Template

Trace 1 onto fusible web

Light Bulb
Template

Trace 20 onto fusible web

Scarf
Template
(cut on bias)

Trace 1 onto fusible web

Light Bulb
Base Template

Trace 20 onto fusible web

Snowman Template

Trace 1 onto fusible web

Button
Template

Trace 5 onto fusible web

Stitching the Cord

Refer to the quilt and position 2 strands of #5 gold pearl cotton along the border to connect and weave through the lights, touching the base of each light.

NOTE: Before stitching on the quilt, practice this technique on a fabric scrap. Set the sewing machine zigzag stitch to the widest width and medium length. Using black thread, zigzag-stitch over the pearl cotton.

Putting It All Together

Trim the backing and batting 4 inches larger than the quilt top.

Refer to **Finishing the Quilt** on page 221 for complete instructions.

Binding the Quilt

Refer to **Binding and Diagonal Piecing** on page 221 for complete instructions with detailed illustrations.

NOTE: The 2-3/4-inch strips will produce a 1/2-inch wide finished double binding. If you would like a wider or narrower binding, adjust the width of the strips.

Cutting

From **RED PRINT** cut
- 3—2-3/4 x 42-inch strips.

Sew the binding to the quilt using a 3/8-inch seam allowance.

Frosty Lights

Holiday Bouquet

Reminiscent of an antique quilt, this beautifully pieced and appliquéd wall hanging uses contrasting colors to show off its dynamic design.

Holiday Bouquet

Quilt measures 54 inches square.
Block measures 14 inches square.

Fabric & Supplies

1-1/8 yards	**BEIGE PRINT #1** for appliqué foundation blocks and Flying Geese units
1/2 yard	**RED PRINT** for Flying Geese units, flower center appliqués, and large leaf appliqués
1 yard	**GREEN PRINT #1** for center square and large leaf and swag appliqués
1-7/8 yards	**BEIGE PRINT #2** for outer border
5/8 yard	**GREEN PRINT #2** for inner border and small leaf appliqués
1/4 yard	**RED FLORAL** for outer flower appliqués
1/4 yard	**GOLD PRINT** for inner flower appliqués and small leaf appliqués
5/8 yard	**RED PRINT** for binding
3-1/4 yards	Backing fabric
Quilt batting	58 inches square

Freezer paper for flower, leaf, and swag appliqués

Lightweight cardboard for flower center appliqués

NOTE: read **Getting Started**,
page 216, before beginning this project.

Flying Geese Units

Make 28 Units

Cutting

From **BEIGE PRINT #1** cut
- 4—2-1/2 x 42-inch strips; from the strips cut 56—2-1/2-inch squares.

From **RED PRINT** cut
- 4—2-1/2 x 42-inch strips; from the strips cut 28—2-1/2 x 4-1/2-inch rectangles.

Piecing

1. Position a 2-1/2-inch BEIGE PRINT #1 square on the corner of a 2-1/2 x 4-1/2-inch RED PRINT rectangle. Draw a diagonal line on the BEIGE PRINT square and stitch on the line. Trim the seam allowance to 1/4 inch; press. Repeat this process at the opposite corner of the RED PRINT rectangle.

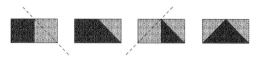

Make 28

2. Sew together 7 of the Step 1 Flying Geese units; press. <u>At this point each Flying Geese strip should measure 4-1/2 x 14-1/2 inches.</u>

Make 4

Foundation Blocks and Appliqué

Cutting

From **BEIGE PRINT #1** cut
- 2—14-1/2 x 42-inch strips; from the strips cut 4—14-1/2-inch appliqué foundation squares.

Diagonally fold each 14-1/2-inch BEIGE PRINT #1 appliqué foundation square in half and press the fold. Diagonally fold the square in half in the opposite direction and press the fold. Use the pressed lines as a guide to position the appliqué shapes.

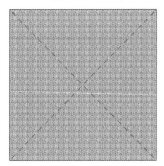

Make 4

Freezer Paper Method
Prepare the Leaves, Outer Flowers, and Swags

With this method of hand appliqué, the freezer paper forms a base to shape the outer flower, large leaf, small leaf, and swag appliqués.

1. Lay the freezer paper, paper side up, on the appliqué shapes. Trace the shapes and cut out along the traced lines.

2. With a dry iron on wool setting, press the coated side of the freezer paper shapes to the wrong side of the fabrics, allowing 3/4 inch between each shape. Cut out the shapes 1/4 inch beyond the edge of the freezer paper and finger-press the edge of the fabric over the edge of the freezer paper.

3. Allowing 3/4-inch space between each shape, position the freezer paper shapes, coated side down, on the wrong side of the fabrics selected for leaves, outer flower, and swag. Use a hot, dry iron to press the shapes to the fabric. Let the fabric cool. Cut out each fabric shape a scant 1/4 inch beyond the edge of the freezer paper and leave the freezer paper in place. Set aside the swag and the RED PRINT and GOLD PRINT leaves to use for the outer border.

4. Referring to the quilt illustration and using the fold lines on the 14-1/2-inch BEIGE PRINT #1 foundation squares, position and pin 4 large GREEN PRINT #1 leaf appliqués. Position 8 small GREEN PRINT #2 leaves, and a RED FLORAL outer flower on each foundation square. Baste all the shapes in place.

5. Beginning with a large leaf, use your needle to turn under the seam allowance toward the freezer paper. Allowing an opening to tuck a small leaf along the base of the left edge of the large leaf, appliqué the leaf in place with matching thread. At the opening for the small leaf, slide the needle into the opening, carefully loosen the freezer paper from the fabric, and gently pull out the paper.

6. Tuck an edge of the small leaf in the opening of the large leaf and appliqué it in place. When there is approximately 3/4 inch remaining to appliqué, use your needle to loosen and remove the freezer paper, as for the large leaf, and finish stitching the leaf in place. Overlap a small leaf on the opposite side of the large leaf and appliqué in place, removing the freezer paper as for the large and small leaves.

7. Appliqué the large outer flower in place, removing the freezer paper as for the leaves.

Cardboard Appliqué Method
Prepare the Inner Flowers and Flower Centers

1. Trace the inner flower and flower center patterns, pages 49–50, onto lightweight cardboard to make templates for each shape.

2. Place the inner flower cardboard template on the wrong side of the GOLD PRINT fabric. Allowing 3/4-inch space between each shape, trace the template 4 times. Cut out the shapes 1/4 inch beyond the traced lines.

3. Place the flower center cardboard template on the wrong side of the RED PRINT fabric. Allowing 3/4-inch space between each shape, trace the template 4 times. Cut out the shapes 1/4 inch beyond the traced lines.

4. To make smooth round circles, sew a line of small basting stitches halfway between the drawn line and the cut edge of the circle; keep the needle and thread attached. Place the appropriate-size cardboard template on the wrong side of the fabric circle, tug on the basting stitches to gather the fabric, evenly space the gathers, securely knot the thread, and clip the thread. Press the circle on both sides and remove the template.

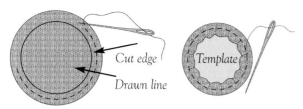

Make 4 Gold Inner Flowers and 4 Red Flower Centers

5. Pin and baste the flower centers to the inner flowers and use matching thread to hand-appliqué the centers in place.

6. Layer the flower units on the appliquéd outer flowers on the foundation squares and hand-appliqué them in place.

Quilt Center

Cutting

From **GREEN PRINT #1** cut
- 1—4-1/2-inch square.

Quilt Center Assembly

1. Refer to the quilt illustration for block placement and sew an appliquéd block to both sides of a Flying Geese strip. Press the seam allowances toward the appliquéd blocks. Make 2 block rows. <u>At this point each block row should measure 14-1/2 x 32-1/2 inches.</u>

2. Refer to the quilt illustration for block placement and sew Flying Geese strips to both sides of the 4-1/2-inch GREEN PRINT #1 square. Press the seam allowances toward the GREEN PRINT #1 square. <u>At this point the Flying Geese strip should measure 4-1/2 x 32-1/2 inches.</u>

3. Sew the Step 1 block rows to both sides of the Step 2 Flying Geese strip; press.

Borders

Refer to **Binding and Diagonal Piecing**, page 221 for complete instructions.

NOTE: The yardage given allows for the border strips to be cut on the crosswise grain.

Cutting

From **GREEN PRINT #2** cut
- 4—1-1/2 x 42-inch strips for the inner border.

From **BEIGE PRINT #2** cut
- 6—10-1/2 x 42-inch strips for the outer border.

Attaching the Borders

1. Measure the quilt from left to right through the center to determine the length of the top and bottom inner border strips. Measure and mark the border lengths and center points on the 1-1/2-inch wide GREEN PRINT #2 inner border strips. Cut 2 strips a few inches longer than needed and pin them to the top and bottom of the quilt. Sew the strips to the quilt and press the seam allowances toward the border. Trim off excess fabric from the ends of the border strips.

2. Measure the quilt from top to bottom through the center, including the border strips just added, to determine the length of the side inner border strips. Measure and mark the border lengths and center points on the 1-1/2-inch wide GREEN PRINT #2 inner border strips. Cut 2 strips a few inches longer than needed and pin them to the sides of the quilt. Sew the strips to the quilt and press the seam allowances toward the border. Trim off excess fabric from the ends of the border strips.

3. To attach the 10-1/2-inch wide BEIGE PRINT #2 outer border strips to the quilt, refer to Step 1, and Step 2.

Appliquéing the Border

1. Refer to the quilt illustration and photograph to position the prepared large leaf, small leaf, and swag appliqués on the border, overlapping shapes as shown. Pin and baste the shapes in place.

2. Beginning with the swag, use your needle to turn under the seam allowance toward the freezer paper. Use matching thread to hand-appliqué the leaf in place. When there is about 3/4 inch remaining to stitch, loosen the freezer paper with the needle and gently remove it from the shape. Complete the stitching.

3. Appliqué the small leaves and the large leaves, removing the freezer paper as for the swag.

Putting It All Together

Cut the 3-1/4 yard length of backing fabric in half crosswise to make 2, 1-5/8 yard lengths.

Refer to **Finishing the Quilt** on page 221 for complete instructions.

Binding the Quilt

Refer to **Binding and Diagonal Piecing** on page 221 for complete instructions with detailed illustrations.

NOTE: The 2-3/4-inch strips will produce a 1/2-inch wide finished double binding. If you would like a wider or narrower binding, adjust the width of the strips.

Cutting

From **RED PRINT** cut
- 6—2-3/4 x 42-inch strips.

Sew the binding to the quilt using a 3/8-inch seam allowance.

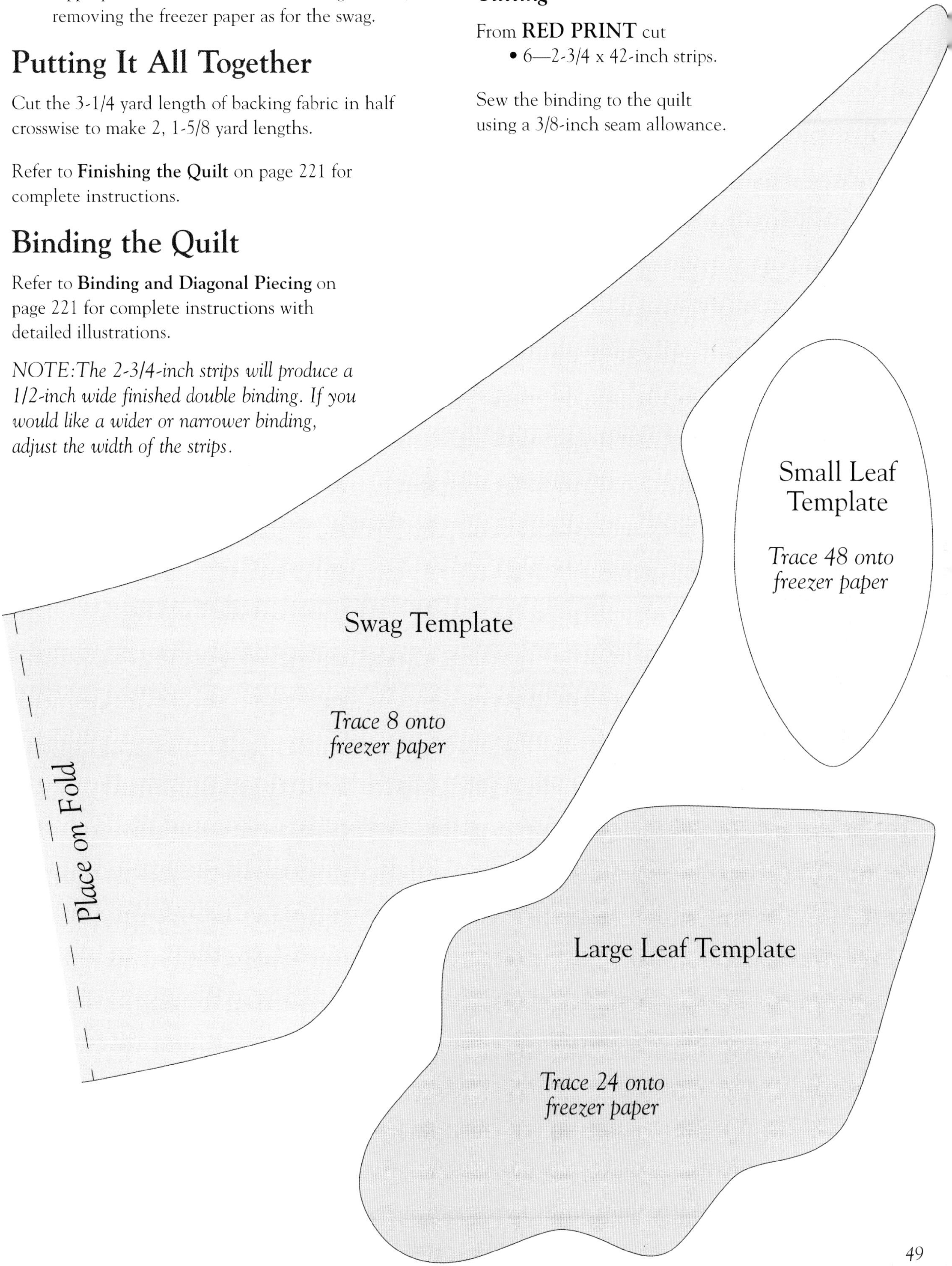

Small Leaf Template

Trace 48 onto freezer paper

Swag Template

Trace 8 onto freezer paper

Place on Fold

Large Leaf Template

Trace 24 onto freezer paper

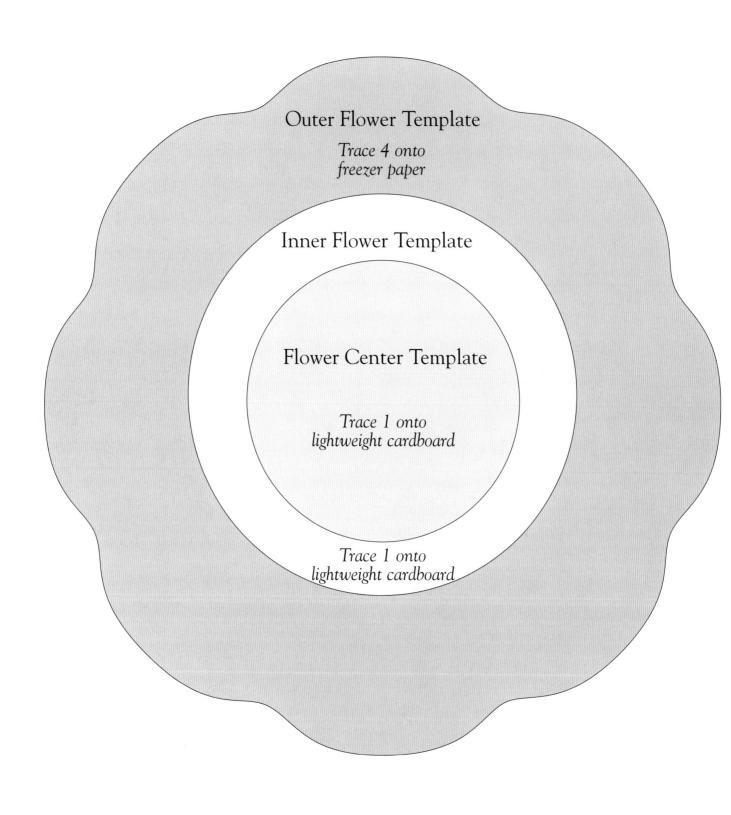

Outer Flower Template

*Trace 4 onto
freezer paper*

Inner Flower Template

Flower Center Template

*Trace 1 onto
lightweight cardboard*

*Trace 1 onto
lightweight cardboard*

Holiday Bouquet

Harvest Time

The best of the season
showcases harvest
pumpkins and autumn
leaves in a palette of warm
country colors ranging
from toasty browns to deep
shades of goldenrod.

Harvest Time

Quilt measures 64 x 70 inches square.

Fabric & Supplies

3/4 yard	**ORANGE PRINT #1** for pumpkins
1/2 yard	**ORANGE PRINT #2** for pumpkins
2-1/4 yards	**BEIGE PRINT** for background and borders
1/2 yard	**DARK BROWN PRINT** for pumpkin stems and pieced border
2/3 yard	**GREEN PRINT #1** for 8 leaves and sawtooth border
1/2 yard	**BROWN PRINT** for 8 leaves
1/4 yard	**GREEN PRINT #2** for 2 leaves
1/3 yard	**GOLD PRINT** for 6 leaves
1-1/2 yards	**CHESTNUT FRUIT PRINT** for outer border
2/3 yard	**GREEN PRINT #1** for binding
3-3/4 yards	Backing fabric
Quilt batting	68 x 74 inches

NOTE: read **Getting Started**,
page 216, before beginning this project.

Pumpkin Blocks

Make 5 Blocks

Cutting

From **ORANGE PRINT #1** cut
- 2—4-1/2 x 42-inch strips; from the strips cut 5—4-1/2 x 12-1/2-inch rectangles.
- 5—2-1/2 x 42-inch strips; from the strips cut 10—2-1/2 x 12-1/2-inch rectangles and 20—2-1/2-inch squares.

From **ORANGE PRINT #2** cut
- 5—2-1/2 x 42-inch strips; from the strips cut 10—2-1/2 x 12-1/2-inch rectangles and 20—2-1/2-inch squares.

From **BEIGE PRINT** cut
- 1—5-1/2 x 42-inch strip; from the strip cut 5—5-1/2 x 6-1/2-inch rectangles.
- 2—3-1/2 x 42-inch strips; from the strips cut 10—3-1/2 x 5-1/2-inch rectangles and 5—3-1/2-inch squares.
- 2—2-1/2 x 42-inch strips; from the strips cut 20—2-1/2-inch squares.

From **DARK BROWN PRINT** cut
- 1—3-1/2 x 42-inch strip; from the strip cut 5—3-1/2 x 5-1/2-inch rectangles and 5—2-1/2 x 3-1/2-inch rectangles.

Piecing

1. Position a 2-1/2-inch ORANGE PRINT #2 square on the corner of a 4-1/2 x 12-1/2-inch ORANGE PRINT #1 rectangle. Draw a diagonal line on the ORANGE PRINT #2 square and stitch on the line. Trim the seam allowance to 1/4 inch; press. Repeat this process on the remaining 3 corners of the ORANGE PRINT #1 rectangle.

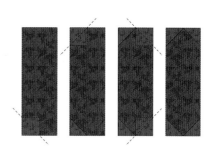

Make 5

2. Position 2-1/2-inch ORANGE PRINT #1 squares on the corners of a 2-1/2 x 12-1/2-inch ORANGE PRINT #2 rectangle. Draw a diagonal line on the ORANGE PRINT #1 squares and stitch on the lines. Trim the seam allowances to 1/4 inch; press.

Make 10

3. Position 2-1/2-inch BEIGE PRINT squares on the corners of a 2-1/2 x 12-1/2-inch ORANGE PRINT #1 rectangle. Draw a diagonal line on the BEIGE PRINT squares and stitch on the lines. Trim the seam allowances to 1/4 inch; press.

Make 10

4. Referring to the illustration, sew together the units from Steps 1, 2, and 3 to complete 5 blocks; press. <u>At this point each pumpkin should measure 12-1/2-inches square.</u>

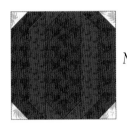

Make 5

5. Sew together in pairs the 2-1/2 x 3-1/2-inch DARK BROWN PRINT rectangles and the 3-1/2 x 5-1/2-inch BEIGE PRINT rectangles to make 5 units; press.

 Make 5

6. Position a 3-1/2 x 5-1/2-inch DARK BROWN PRINT rectangle on the right corner of a 3-1/2 x 5-1/2-inch BEIGE PRINT rectangle, referring to the illustration. Draw a diagonal line on the BROWN PRINT rectangle and stitch on the line. Trim the seam allowance to 1/4 inch; press.

Make 5

7. Referring to the illustration for placement, position a 3-1/2-inch BEIGE PRINT square on the right corner of each of the Step 6 units. Draw

a diagonal line on the BEIGE PRINT square and stitch on the line. Trim the seam allowance to 1/4 inch; press.

Make 5

8. Sew each Step 7 unit to the top of each Step 5 unit; press. Sew a 5-1/2 x 6-1/2-inch BEIGE PRINT rectangle to the right-hand side of each of these units; press. <u>At this point each pumpkin stem unit should measure 6-1/2 x 12-1/2 inches.</u>

Make 5

NOTE: *If the pumpkin base does not match the stem unit, recheck your measurements and seam allowances. Because so many seams are involved, there is a tendency for the pumpkin base to be a bit smaller than the stem unit. For this reason, it is necessary to recheck seam allowances and make necessary adjustments. DO NOT trim down the stem unit.*

9. Sew the stem units to the top of the pumpkin units; press. <u>At this point each pumpkin block should measure 12-1/2 x 18-1/2 inches.</u>

Make 5

Leaf Blocks

Make 8 from **GREEN PRINT #1**
Make 8 from **BROWN PRINT**
Make 6 from **GOLD PRINT**
Make 2 from **GREEN PRINT #2**
  for a total of 24 Leaf Blocks

Cutting

From **GREEN PRINT #1** cut
- 3—4-1/2 x 42-inch strips; from the strips cut
  8—4-1/2-inch squares,
  16—2-1/2 x 4-1/2-inch rectangles, and
  8—1 x 4-1/2-inch rectangles for stems.

From **BROWN PRINT** cut
- 3—4-1/2 x 42-inch strips; from the strips cut
  8—4-1/2-inch squares,
  16—2-1/2 x 4-1/2-inch rectangles, and
  8—1 x 4-1/2-inch rectangles for stems.

From **GOLD PRINT** cut
- 2—4-1/2 x 42-inch strips; from the strips cut
  6—4-1/2-inch squares,
  12—2-1/2 x 4-1/2-inch rectangles, and
  6—1 x 4-1/2-inch rectangles for stems.

From **GREEN PRINT #2** cut
- 1—4-1/2 x 42-inch strip; from the strip cut
  2—4-1/2-inch squares.
  4—2-1/2 x 4-1/2-inch rectangles, and
  2—1 x 4-1/2-inch rectangles for stems.

From **BEIGE PRINT** cut
- 6—2-1/2 x 42-inch strips; from the strips cut
  96—2-1/2-inch squares
- 2—2-5/8 x 42-inch strips; from the strips cut
  24—2-5/8-inch squares. Cut the squares in
  half diagonally to make 48 triangles for the
  stem units.

Piecing

1. To make the GREEN PRINT #1 leaves, position 2-1/2-inch BEIGE PRINT squares on opposite corners of 4-1/2-inch GREEN PRINT #1 squares. Draw a diagonal line on the BEIGE PRINT squares and stitch on the lines. Trim the seam allowances to 1/4 inch; press.

Make 8 from GREEN PRINT #1

2. Position a 2-1/2-inch BEIGE PRINT square on the right-hand corner of a 2-1/2 x 4-1/2-inch GREEN PRINT #1 rectangle. Draw a diagonal line on the BEIGE PRINT square and stitch on the line. Trim the seam allowance to 1/4 inch; press.

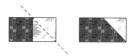

Make 8 from GREEN PRINT #1

3. Position a 2-1/2-inch BEIGE PRINT square on the left-hand corner of a 2-1/2 x 4-1/2-inch GREEN PRINT #1 rectangle. Draw a diagonal line on the BEIGE PRINT square and stitch on the line. Trim the seam allowance to 1/4 inch; press.

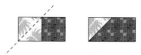

Make 8 from GREEN PRINT #1

4. For the stem units, center BEIGE PRINT triangles on each of the 1 x 4-1/2-inch GREEN PRINT #1 rectangles, as shown. Stitch a 1/4-inch seam allowance. Press the seam allowance toward the GREEN PRINT #1 rectangle. Center another BEIGE PRINT triangle on each GREEN PRINT #1 strip; stitch and press. The stems will extend beyond the triangles. Trim the ends of each stem so that each unit measures 2-1/2 inches square.

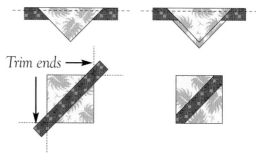

Make 8 from GREEN PRINT #1

5. Sew the stem units to the left-hand side of the Step 2 leaf units; press.

Make 8 from GREEN PRINT #1

56

6. Sew the Step 3 leaf units to the left-hand side of the Step 1 leaf units; press.

Make 8 from GREEN PRINT #1

7. Referring to the block illustration, sew together the Step 5 and the Step 6 units; press. <u>At this point each leaf block should measure 6-1/2 inches square.</u>

Make 8 from GREEN PRINT #1

8. Follow Steps 1 through 7 to make the remaining leaves:

Make 6 using GOLD PRINT *Make 8 using BROWN PRINT* *Make 2 using GREEN PRINT #2*

Quilt Center

Quilt Center Assembly

Refer to the illustration to sew together 12 leaf blocks and the pumpkin blocks in 3 vertical rows. Sew the rows together; press. <u>At this point, the quilt center should measure 36-1/2 x 42-1/2 inches.</u>

Quilt Center

Borders

Refer to **Binding and Diagonal Piecing**, page 221 for complete instructions.

NOTE: The yardage given allows for the border strips to be cut on the crosswise grain.

Cutting

From **GREEN PRINT #1** cut

- 2—2-7/8 x 42-inch strips for the sawtooth border.

From **BEIGE PRINT** cut

- 2—2-7/8 x 42-inch strips for the sawtooth border.
- 4—2-1/2 x 42-inch strips; from the strips cut 2—2-1/2 x 24-1/2-inch strips for the top and bottom inner pieced border and 2—2-1/2 x 30-1/2-inch strips for the side inner pieced border.
- 6—2-1/2 x 42-inch strips for the middle border.

From **DARK BROWN PRINT** cut

- 4—2-1/2 x 42-inch strips; from the strips cut 2—2-1/2 x 24-1/2-inch strips for the top and bottom inner pieced border and 2—2-1/2 x 30-1/2-inch strips for the side inner pieced border.

From **CHESTNUT FRUIT PRINT** cut

- 7—6-1/2 x 42-inch strips for the outer border.

Piecing and Attaching the Borders

1. Layer the 2-7/8 x 42-inch BEIGE PRINT and GREEN PRINT #1 strips in pairs. Press, but do not sew, the strips together. Crosscut the layered strips into 27, 2-7/8-inch squares.

Crosscut 27, 2-7/8-inch squares

2. Cut the layered squares in half diagonally. Stitch 1/4 inch from the diagonal edge of each pair of triangles; press the unit open. <u>At this point each triangle-pieced square should measure 2-1/2 inches square.</u>

Make 54, 2-1/2-inch triangle-pieced squares

3. For the top and bottom sawtooth border strips, sew together 12 triangle-pieced squares; press. <u>At this point each sawtooth border strip should measure 2-1/2 x 24-1/2 inches.</u> Sew a 2-1/2 x 24-1/2-inch BEIGE PRINT strip to the bottom of each sawtooth border strip; press. Sew a 2-1/2 x 24-1/2-inch DARK BROWN PRINT strip to the top of each sawtooth border strip; press.

Make 2

4. Sew a GOLD PRINT leaf block to the right-hand side of the top and bottom pieced border strips; press. Sew a BROWN PRINT leaf block to the left-hand side of the pieced border strips; press. Sew a border strip to the top of the quilt center; press. Sew a border strip to the bottom of the quilt center; press.

5. For the side sawtooth border strips, sew together 15 triangle-pieced squares; press. <u>At this point each sawtooth border strip should measure 2-1/2 x 30-1/2 inches.</u> Sew a 2-1/2 x 30-1/2-inch BEIGE PRINT strip to the top of each sawtooth border strip; press. Sew a 2-1/2 x 30-1/2-inch DARK BROWN PRINT strip to the bottom of each sawtooth border strip; press.

6. Sew a GOLD PRINT leaf block to the left-hand side of the pieced border strips; press. Sew a BROWN PRINT leaf block to the right-hand side of the pieced border strips; press.

7. Referring to the illustration, sew GREEN PRINT #1 leaf blocks to both ends of the pieced border strips; press. Sew the border strips to the sides of the quilt center; press.

Make 2

8. Measure the quilt from left to right through the center to determine the length of the top and bottom middle border strips. Cut 2, 2-1/2-inch

wide BEIGE PRINT strips to this measurement. Sew the border strips to the quilt; press.

9. Measure the quilt from top to bottom through the center, including the border strips just added, to determine the length of the side middle border strips. Cut 2, 2-1/2-inch wide BEIGE PRINT strips to this measurement. Sew the border strips to the quilt; press.

10. Measure the quilt from left to right through the center to determine the length of the top and bottom outer border strips. Cut 2, 6-1/2-inch wide CHESTNUT FRUIT PRINT strips to this measurement. Sew the border strips to the quilt; press.

11. Measure the quilt from top to bottom through the center, including the borders just added, to determine the length of the side outer border strips. Cut 2, 6-1/2-inch wide CHESTNUT FRUIT PRINT strips to this measurement. Sew the border strips to the quilt; press.

Putting It All Together

Cut the 3-3/4 yard length of backing fabric in half crosswise to make 2, 1-7/8 yard lengths.

Refer to **Finishing the Quilt** on page 221 for complete instructions.

Binding the Quilt

Refer to **Binding and Diagonal Piecing** on page 221 for complete instructions with detailed illustrations.

NOTE: The 2-3/4-inch strips will produce a 1/2-inch wide finished double binding. If you would like a wider or narrower binding, adjust the width of the strips.

Cutting

From **GREEN PRINT #1** cut
- 7—2-3/4 x 42-inch strips.

Sew the binding to the quilt using a 3/8-inch seam allowance.

Harvest Time

Holly Hill Town

A winter village scene evokes
nostalgic memories of small town
America—complete with
white picket fences.
Wide borders artfully frame the
pictorial center scene.

House Blocks

Make 2 Small Houses and 1 Large House

Cutting

From **GOLD PRINT #2** cut
- 1—2-1/2 x 3-1/2-inch rectangle.
- 1—2-1/2 x 5-1/2-inch rectangle.
- 1—1-1/2 x 42-inch strip; from the strip cut
  3—1-1/2 x 8-inch strips,
  2—1-1/2 x 5-1/2-inch rectangles, and
  2—1-1/2 x 3-1/2-inch rectangles.
- 1—3-1/2 x 6-1/2-inch rectangle.

From **RED PRINT** cut
- 1—2-1/2 x 3-1/2-inch rectangle.
- 2—1-1/2 x 42-inch strips; from the strips cut
  3—1-1/2 x 10-inch strips,
  4—1-1/2 x 5-1/2-inch rectangles, and
  2—1-1/2 x 3-1/2-inch rectangles.

From **BLACK PRINT** cut
- 1—1-1/2 x 42-inch strip; from the strip cut
  2—1-1/2 x 8-inch strips and
  2—1-1/2 x 10-inch strips.
- 1—3-1/2 x 26-inch strip; from the strip cut
  1—3-1/2-inch square,
  2—3-1/2 x 6-1/2-inch rectangles, and
  1—3-1/2 x 7-1/2-inch rectangle.

From **WHEAT PRINT** cut
- 6—3-1/2-inch squares.

Piecing

1. To make the roofs for the small houses, position a 3-1/2-inch WHEAT PRINT square on the corner of a 3-1/2 x 6-1/2-inch BLACK PRINT rectangle. Draw a diagonal line on the WHEAT PRINT square and stitch on the line. Trim the seam allowance to 1/4 inch; press. Repeat this process at the opposite corner of the BLACK PRINT rectangle; press.

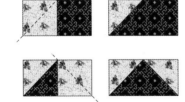

Make 2

2. To make the front roof unit for the large house, position a 3-1/2-inch WHEAT PRINT square on the left-hand corner of the 3-1/2 x 6-1/2-inch GOLD PRINT #2 rectangle. Draw a diagonal line on the WHEAT PRINT square and stitch on the line. Trim the seam allowance to 1/4 inch; press. Repeat this process at the opposite corner of the GOLD PRINT #2 rectangle using the 3-1/2-inch BLACK PRINT square.

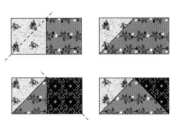

Make 1

3. To make the side roof unit, position a 3-1/2-inch WHEAT PRINT square on the right-hand corner of the 3-1/2 x 7-1/2-inch BLACK PRINT rectangle. Draw a diagonal line on the WHEAT PRINT square and stitch on the line. Trim the seam allowance to 1/4 inch; press.

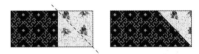

Make 1

4. To make the red double-window units, sew the 3, 1-1/2 x 10-inch RED PRINT strips and the 2, 1-1/2 x 10-inch BLACK PRINT strips together; press. Crosscut the strip set into 5, 1-1/2-inch segments. From 2 of the segments, remove a BLACK PRINT and a RED PRINT square from one end to use for the windows for the small house.

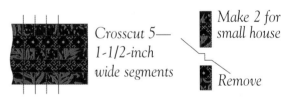

Crosscut 5— 1-1/2-inch wide segments

Make 2 for small house

Remove

5. Sew the 4, 1-1/2 x 5-1/2-inch RED PRINT rectangles and the 3 double-window units (from Step 4) together; press. Sew the side roof unit (Step 3) to the top of the unit; press.

Make 1

6. To make the gold double-window units, sew the 3, 1-1/2 x 8-inch GOLD PRINT #2 strips and the 2, 1-1/2 x 8-inch BLACK PRINT strips together; press. From the strip sets, crosscut 4, 1-1/2-inch segments. From 2 of the segments, remove a BLACK PRINT and a GOLD PRINT #2 square from one end. Use these 2 segments for the small house.

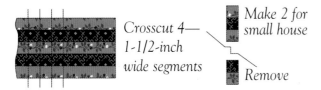

Crosscut 4— 1-1/2-inch wide segments

Make 2 for small house

Remove

7. Sew the 2, 1-1/2 x 5-1/2-inch GOLD PRINT #2 rectangles, the 2-1/2 x 5-1/2-inch GOLD PRINT #2 rectangle, and the 2 double-window units together; press. Sew the roof unit from Step 2 to the top of this unit; press. Sew the unit from Step 5 to the right side of this unit; press.

 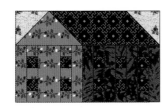

Make 1

8. Sew the 2, 1-1/2 x 3-1/2-inch RED PRINT rectangles, the 2-1/2 x 3-1/2-inch RED PRINT rectangle, and the 2 single-window units together; press. Sew a roof unit from Step 1 to the top of this unit; press. Repeat this process using the GOLD PRINT #2 rectangles and the GOLD PRINT #2 single-window units from Step 6 to make a small GOLD PRINT #2 house. Sew the houses together.

Church Block

Cutting

From **BEIGE PRINT** cut
- 1—2-1/2 x 42-inch strip; from the strip cut
  2—2-1/2 x 7-1/2-inch rectangles,

1—2-1/2 x 5-1/2-inch rectangle,
1—2-1/2-inch square,
4—1-1/2 x 2-1/2-inch rectangles, and
6—1-1/2-inch squares.

From **WHEAT PRINT** cut
- 2—3-1/2 x 5-1/2-inch rectangles.
- 1—3-1/2 x 4-1/2-inch rectangle.
- 1—4-1/2-inch square.
- 2—1-1/2 x 6-1/2-inch rectangles.
- 2—1-1/2 x 2-1/2-inch rectangles.
- 2—1-1/2-inch squares.
- 2—2-1/2-inch squares.

From **BLACK PRINT** cut
- 3—2-1/2 x 4-1/2-inch rectangles.
- 1—2-1/2 x 5-1/2-inch rectangle.
- 2—3-1/2-inch squares.
- 2—1-1/2 x 3-1/2-inch rectangles.

Piecing

1. Position a 2-1/2-inch WHEAT PRINT square on the corner of a 2-1/2 x 4-1/2-inch BLACK PRINT rectangle. Draw a diagonal line on the WHEAT PRINT square and stitch on the line. Trim seam allowance to 1/4 inch; press. Repeat this process at the opposite corner of the BLACK PRINT rectangle; press.

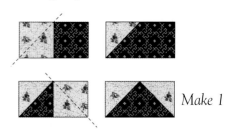

Make 1

2. Sew a 1-1/2 x 2-1/2-inch WHEAT PRINT rectangle to both sides of the 2-1/2-inch BEIGE PRINT square; press. Sew the roof unit from Step 1 to the top of this unit; press. Sew the 4-1/2-inch WHEAT PRINT square to the left side and the 3-1/2 x 4-1/2-inch WHEAT PRINT rectangle to the right side; press.

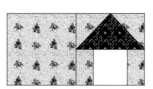

Make 1

3. Position 1-1/2-inch BEIGE PRINT squares on the left corners of the 2-1/2 x 4-1/2-inch BLACK PRINT rectangles and the 2-1/2 x 5-1/2-inch BLACK PRINT rectangle. Draw a diagonal line on the BEIGE PRINT squares and stitch on the line. Trim the seam allowances to 1/4 inch; press. Repeat this process at the adjacent corners of the BLACK PRINT rectangles; press.

Make 2   Make 1

4. Sew 1-1/2 x 2-1/2-inch BEIGE PRINT rectangles to the top and bottom of the window units; press. Sew one 1-1/2 x 6-1/2-inch WHEAT PRINT rectangle to each of the window units; press.

Window units

5. Position 1-1/2-inch WHEAT PRINT squares on one left and one right corner of the 1-1/2 x 3-1/2-inch BLACK PRINT rectangles. Draw a diagonal line on the WHEAT PRINT squares and stitch on the line. Trim the seam allowances to 1/4 inch; press. Sew these units to the top of the units from Step 4 (see Step 6 diagram); press.

Make 1   Make 1

6. Sew one 2-1/2 x 7-1/2-inch BEIGE PRINT rectangle to each of these units; press.

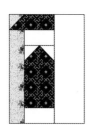 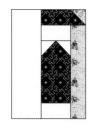

7. Position 3-1/2-inch BLACK PRINT squares on one right and one left corner of the 3-1/2 x 5-1/2-inch WHEAT PRINT rectangles. Draw a diagonal line on the BLACK PRINT squares and stitch on the line. Trim the seam allowances to

1/4 inch; press. Sew these roof units to the top of the units made in Step 6; press.

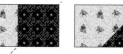

Make 1   *Make 1*

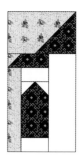 

8. Sew the 2-1/2 x 5-1/2-inch BEIGE PRINT rectangle to the top of the remaining door unit from Step 3; press. Sew the units from Step 7 to both sides of this unit; press.

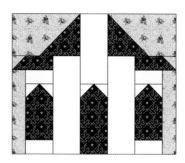

Church block

Walkway

Cutting

From **BROWN PRINT** cut
- 1—2-1/2 x 6-1/2-inch rectangle
- 4—1-1/2-inch squares.

From **WHEAT PRINT** cut
- 2—1-1/2 x 2-1/2-inch rectangles
- 4—1-1/2-inch squares.

Piecing

Sew one 1-1/2 x 2-1/2-inch WHEAT PRINT rectangle, 2, 1-1/2-inch WHEAT PRINT squares, and 2, 1-1/2-inch BROWN PRINT squares together; press. Make a total of 2 and sew them to the sides of the 2-1/2 x 6-1/2-inch BROWN PRINT rectangle; press.

Make 1

Fence Sections

Cutting

From **BEIGE PRINT** cut
- 2—1-1/2 x 42-inch strips; from the strips cut 16—1-1/2 x 4-1/2-inch rectangles.
- 1—1-1/2 x 42-inch strip.

From **WHEAT PRINT** cut
- 1—3-1/2 x 6-1/2-inch rectangle.
- 1—2-1/2 x 42-inch strip.
- 1—1-1/2 x 42-inch strip.
- 16—1-1/2-inch squares.

Piecing

1. Position 1-1/2-inch WHEAT PRINT squares at the top edge of the 1-1/2 x 4-1/2-inch BEIGE PRINT rectangles. Draw a diagonal line on the WHEAT PRINT squares and stitch on the line. Trim the seam allowances to 1/4 inch; press. Make 9 of these fence units with the points on the right side; reverse the direction of the diagonal line on the remaining 7 to create points on the left side.

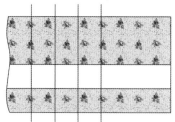

Make 9 *Make 7*

2. Sew the 2-1/2 x 42-inch WHEAT PRINT strip and the 1-1/2 x 42-inch WHEAT PRINT strip to both sides of the 1-1/2 x 42-inch BEIGE PRINT strip; press. From the strip set, crosscut 13, 1-1/2-inch segments and one 2-1/2-inch segment.

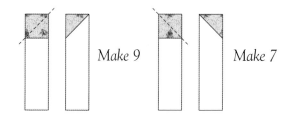

Crosscut 13— 1-1/2-inch wide segments and

1—2-1/2-inch wide segment

3. Sew 2 fence units to both sides of a 1-1/2-inch-wide segment from Step 2; press. Sew the 3-1/2 x 6-1/2-inch WHEAT PRINT rectangle to the top of this unit; press.

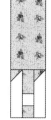

4. Placing the 2-1/2-inch wide segment from Step 2 in the center, sew the remaining fence units and 1-1/2-inch wide segments together; press.

Quilt Center Assembly

Referring to the Assembly Diagram, sew the units together in horizontal rows; press. Sew the horizontal rows together; press.

Borders

Refer to **Binding and Diagonal Piecing**, page 221 for complete instructions.

NOTE: The yardage given allows for the border strips to be cut on the crosswise grain. Diagonally piece the strips as needed.

Cutting

From **WHEAT PRINT** cut
- 1—3-1/2 x 42-inch strip for the bottom background section.

From **RED PRINT** cut
- 4—3-1/2 x 42-inch strips for the inner border.

From **BLACK PRINT** cut
- 4—3-1/2-inch squares for the corner squares.

From **GREEN PRINT #2** cut
- 6—6-1/2 x 42-inch strips for the outer border.

Attaching the Inner Border

1. Measure the quilt from left to right through the center to determine the length of the bottom background section and the top and bottom inner border strips. From the 3-1/2-inch wide WHEAT PRINT strip, cut 1 strip to the length needed and sew it to the bottom of the quilt; press. From the 3-1/2-inch wide RED PRINT strips, cut 2 strips to this length and sew them to the top and bottom of the quilt; press.

2. For the side inner border strips, measure the quilt from top to bottom, including seam allowances but not the RED PRINT inner border strips just added. From the 3-1/2-inch wide RED PRINT strips, cut 2 border strips to the length needed. Sew the 3-1/2-inch BLACK PRINT corner squares to both ends of the border strips; press. Sew the border strips to the quilt; press.

Adding the Appliqué

From **GREEN PRINT #3** cut
- 2—1-3/4 x 7-inch strips for the stems.

1. Fold the GREEN PRINT #3 strips in half lengthwise, wrong sides together; press. To keep the raw edges aligned, stitch a scant 1/4 inch away from the raw edges. Fold the strips in half again so the raw edges are hidden by the first folded edge; press.

2. Trace the leaves and berries onto fusible web, leaving 3/4 inch between each shape. Roughly cut around the shapes 1/4 inch outside the traced lines.

3. Fuse the shapes to the wrong side of the fabrics selected. Cut out the shapes on the marked line, let the fabric cool, and peel away the paper from the fusible web.

4. Referring to the quilt illustration, position the shapes on the quilt. Pin and baste the stems in place. Using matching thread, appliqué the stems. Fuse the leaves and berries in place.

5. Use #8 black pearl cotton to buttonhole-stitch around the edges of the leaves and berries.

Attaching the Outer Border

1. For the top and bottom outer border strips, measure the quilt from left to right through the center. From the 6-1/2-inch wide GREEN PRINT #2 strips, cut 2 border strips to this length and sew them to the top and bottom of the quilt; press.

2. For the side outer border strips, measure the quilt from top to bottom, including the border strips just added. From the 6-1/2-inch wide GREEN PRINT #2 strips, cut 2 border strips to this length and sew them to the quilt; press.

Putting It All Together

Cut the 3 yard length of backing fabric in half crosswise to make 2, 1-1/2 yard lengths.

Refer to **Finishing the Quilt** on page 221 for complete instructions.

Binding the Quilt

Refer to **Binding and Diagonal Piecing** on page 221 for complete instructions with detailed illustrations.

NOTE: *The 2-3/4-inch strips will produce a 1/2-inch wide finished double binding. If you would like a wider or narrower binding, adjust the width of the strips.*

Cutting

From **RED PRINT** cut
- 6—2-3/4 x 42-inch strips.

Sew the binding to the quilt using a 3/8-inch seam allowance.

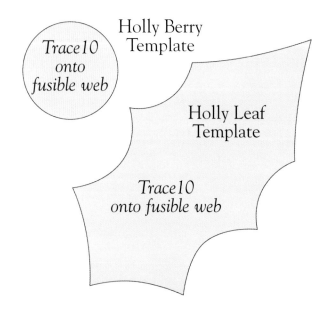

Trace 10 onto fusible web

Holly Berry Template

Holly Leaf Template

Trace 10 onto fusible web

Holly Hill Town

Harvest Apple

This table runner is a great choice for beginning quilters and for gift-giving. Simple, stylized apples work well with almost any decorating style—from country to contemporary.

Harvest Apple

Table runner measures 23 x 39-1/2 inches.

Fabric & Supplies

8-inch squares	**ASSORTED PLAIDS** (10 squares) for patchwork center
1/3 yard	**RED PRINT #1** for inner border
5/8 yard	**CHESTNUT/BLACK PLAID** for outer border
1/4 yard	**TAN/RED PLAID** for corner squares
1/4 yard	**RED PRINT #2** for apple appliqués
6-inch squares	**GREEN PRINTS** (2 squares) for leaf appliqués
4-inch square	**BROWN PRINT** for stem appliqués
3/8 yard	**GREEN PRINT** for binding
1-1/4 yards	Backing fabric
Quilt batting	27 x 44 inches

Paper-backed fusible web or freezer paper

#8 Black pearl cotton for decorative stitches

*NOTE: read **Getting Started**, page 216, before beginning this project.*

Patchwork Center

Cutting

From **ASSORTED PLAIDS** cut
- 10—6-inch squares.

Piecing

1. Sew the PLAID squares together in 2 rows of 5 squares each; press.

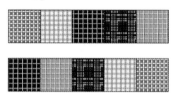

2. Sew the 2 rows together; press.

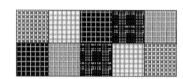

Make 1 patchwork center

Appliqué

Fusible Web Method

1. Position the fusible web, paper side up, on the appliqué shapes. Trace the appliqué shapes on the paper side of the fusible web, leaving a small margin between each shape. Cut the shapes apart, leaving a small margin beyond the drawn lines.

NOTE: When you are fusing a large shape, like the apple, fuse just the outer edges of the shape so that it will not look stiff when finished. To do this, draw a line about 3/8-inch inside the apple, and cut away the fusible web on this line.

2. Place the coated side of the fusible web on the wrong side of the fabrics for the appliqués. Press with a hot, dry iron. Let the fabric cool. Then cut out the shapes on the traced lines. Remove the paper backing from the fusible web.

3. Referring to the illustration and photograph of the runner, position the appliqué shapes on the patchwork center. Fuse the shapes to the patchwork. Allow the fabric to cool.

4. Use #8 black pearl cotton to buttonhole-stitch around the edges of the appliqués.

Freezer Paper Method

Use this method of hand-appliqué for a traditional finished look. The freezer paper forms a base around which the fabric is shaped.

1. Lay the freezer paper, paper side up, on the appliqué shapes. Trace the shapes and cut out along the traced lines.

2. With a dry iron on wool setting, press the coated side of the freezer-paper shapes to the wrong side of the fabrics, allowing 3/4 inch between each shape. Cut out the shapes 1/4 inch beyond the edge of the freezer paper and finger-press the edge of the fabric over the edge of the freezer paper.

3. Position and pin the appliqué shapes to the patchwork center, referring to the runner illustration and photograph. Use matching thread and small slip stitches to appliqué the shape by needle-turning the seam allowance under the edge of the freezer paper. When there is about 3/4 inch remaining to appliqué on each shape, slide the needle into the opening and use it to loosen the freezer paper. Gently remove the paper and finish stitching the shape in place.

Borders

NOTE: *The yardage allows for the border strips to be cut on the crosswise grain.*

Cutting

From **RED PRINT #1** cut
- 3—2-1/2 x 42-inch strips for the inner border.

From **CHESTNUT/BLACK PLAID** cut
- 3—4-1/2 x 42-inch strips for the outer border.

From **TAN/RED PLAID** cut
- 4—4-1/2-inch corner squares.

Attaching the Borders

1. Measure the runner from top to bottom through the center to determine the length of the side inner border strips. Cut 2, 2-1/2-inch wide RED PRINT #1 inner border strips to this measurement and sew them to the sides of the runner; press.

2. Measure the runner from left to right through the center to determine the length of the top and bottom inner border strips. Cut 2, 2-1/2-inch wide RED PRINT #1 inner border strips to this measurement and sew them to the top and bottom of the runner; press.

3. Measure the runner from top to bottom through the center to determine the length of the side outer border strips. Cut 2, 4-1/2-inch wide CHESTNUT/BLACK PLAID outer border strips to this measurement and sew them to the sides of the runner; press.

4. Measure the runner from left to right through the center, including seam allowances but not the side border strips. Cut 2, 4-1/2-inch wide CHESTNUT/BLACK PLAID outer border strips to this measurement. Sew a 4-1/2-inch TAN/RED PLAID corner square to each end of the border strips; press. Sew the border strips to the quilt; press.

Putting It All Together

Trim the backing and batting 4 inches larger than the quilt top.

Refer to **Finishing the Quilt** on page 221 for complete instructions.

Binding the Table Runner

Refer to **Binding and Diagonal Piecing** on page 221 for complete instructions with detailed illustrations.

NOTE: *The 2-3/4-inch strips will produce a 1/2-inch wide finished double binding. If you would like a wider or narrower binding, adjust the width of the strips.*

Cutting

From **GREEN PRINT** cut
- 4—2-3/4 x 42-inch strips.

Sew the binding to the quilt using a 3/8-inch seam allowance.

Pattern Notes

Appliqué Pieces

*The appliqué pieces are reversed images
for tracing onto fusible web or freezer paper.
When the appliqué is finished, it will
appear as it does in the photograph of
the finished quilt.*

Leaf Template

*Trace 2 onto
fusible web/freezer paper*

Leaf Template

*Trace 2 onto
fusible web/freezer paper*

Stem Template

*Trace 2 onto
fusible web/freezer paper*

Apple Template

*Trace 2 onto
fusible web/freezer paper*

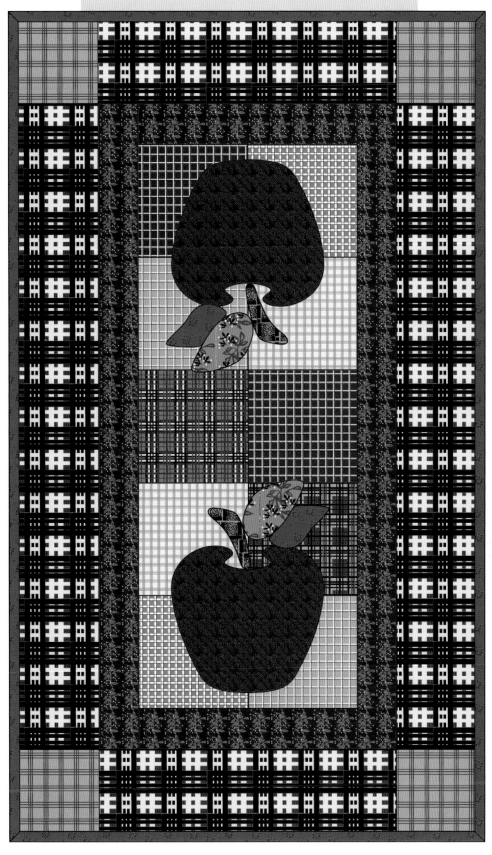

Harvest Apple

Harvest
Pumpkin

Pumpkin motifs take center stage on an easy ten-block table runner that works up quickly for a last-minute autumn accent.

Harvest Pumpkin

Quilt measures 23 x 39-1/2 inches.

Fabric & Supplies

8-inch squares	**ASSORTED PLAIDS** (10 squares) for patchwork center
1/3 yard	**BLACK PRINT #1** for inner border
5/8 yard	**CHESTNUT/BLACK CHECK** for outer border
1/4 yard	**BLACK PRINT #2** for corner squares
1/4 yard	**ORANGE PRINT** for pumpkin appliqués
6-inch squares	**GREEN PRINTS** (3 squares) for leaf appliqués
3-inch square	**BROWN PRINT** for stem appliqués
3/8 yard	**BLACK PRINT #1** for binding
1-1/4 yards	Backing fabric
Quilt batting	27 x 44 inches

Paper-backed fusible web or freezer paper

#8 Black pearl cotton for decorative stitches

*NOTE: read **Getting Started**, page 216, before beginning this project.*

Patchwork Center

Cutting

From **ASSORTED PLAIDS** cut
* 10—6-inch squares.

Piecing

1. Sew the PLAID squares together in 2 rows of 5 squares each; press.

2. Sew the 2 rows together; press.

Make 1 patchwork center

Appliqué

Fusible Web Method

1. Position the fusible web, paper side up, on the appliqué shapes. Trace the appliqué shapes on the paper side of the fusible web, leaving a small margin between each shape. Cut the shapes apart, leaving a small margin beyond the drawn lines.

NOTE: When you are fusing a large shape, like the pumpkin, fuse just the outer edges of the shape so that it will not look stiff when finished. To do this, draw a line about 3/8-inch inside the pumpkin, and cut away the fusible web on this line.

2. Place the coated side of the fusible web on the wrong side of the fabrics for the appliqués. Press with a hot, dry iron. Let the fabric cool. Then cut out the shapes on the traced lines. Remove the paper backing from the fusible web.

3. Referring to the illustration and photograph of the runner, position the appliqué shapes on the patchwork center. Fuse the shapes to the patchwork. Allow the fabric to cool.

4. Use #8 black pearl cotton to buttonhole-stitch around the edges of the appliqués.

Freezer Paper Method

Use this method of hand-appliqué for a traditional finished look. The freezer paper forms a base around which the fabric is shaped.

1. Lay the freezer paper, paper side up, on the appliqué shapes. Trace the shapes and cut out along the traced lines.

2. With a dry iron on wool setting, press the coated side of the freezer-paper shapes to the wrong side of the fabrics, allowing 3/4 inch between each shape. Cut out the shapes 1/4 inch beyond the edge of the freezer paper and finger-press the edge of the fabric over the edge of the freezer paper.

3. Position and pin the appliqué shapes to the patchwork center, referring to the runner illustration and photograph. Use matching thread and small slip stitches to appliqué the shape by needle-turning the seam allowance under the edge of the freezer paper. When there is about 3/4 inch remaining to appliqué on each shape, slide the needle into the opening and use it to loosen the freezer paper. Gently remove the paper and finish stitching the shape in place.

Borders

NOTE: *The yardage allows for the border strips to be cut on the crosswise grain.*

Cutting

From **BLACK PRINT #1** cut
- 3—2-1/2 x 42-inch strips for the inner border.

From **CHESTNUT/BLACK CHECK** cut
- 3—4-1/2 x 42-inch strips for the outer border.

From **BLACK PRINT #2** cut
- 4—4-1/2-inch corner squares.

Attaching the Borders

1. Measure the runner from top to bottom through the center to determine the length of the side inner border strips. Cut 2, 2-1/2-inch wide BLACK PRINT #1 inner border strips to this measurement and sew them to the sides of the runner; press.

2. Measure the runner from left to right through the center to determine the length of the top and bottom inner border strips. Cut 2, 2-1/2-inch wide BLACK PRINT #1 inner border strips to this measurement and sew them to the top and bottom of the runner; press.

3. Measure the runner from top to bottom through the center to determine the length of the side outer border strips. Cut 2, 4-1/2-inch wide CHESTNUT/BLACK CHECK outer border strips to this measurement and sew them to the sides of the runner; press.

4. Measure the runner from left to right through the center, including seam allowances but not the side border strips. Cut 2, 4-1/2-inch wide CHESTNUT/BLACK CHECK outer border strips to this measurement. Sew a 4-1/2-inch BLACK PRINT #2 corner square to each end of the border strips; press. Sew the border strips to the quilt; press.

Putting It All Together

Trim the backing and batting 4 inches larger than the quilt top.

Refer to **Finishing the Quilt** on page 221 for complete instructions.

Binding the Table Runner

Refer to **Binding and Diagonal Piecing** on page 221 for complete instructions with detailed illustrations.

NOTE: *The 2-3/4-inch strips will produce a 1/2-inch wide finished double binding. If you would like a wider or narrower binding, adjust the width of the strips.*

Cutting

From **BLACK PRINT #1** cut
- 4—2-3/4 x 42-inch strips.

Sew the binding to the quilt using a 3/8-inch seam allowance.

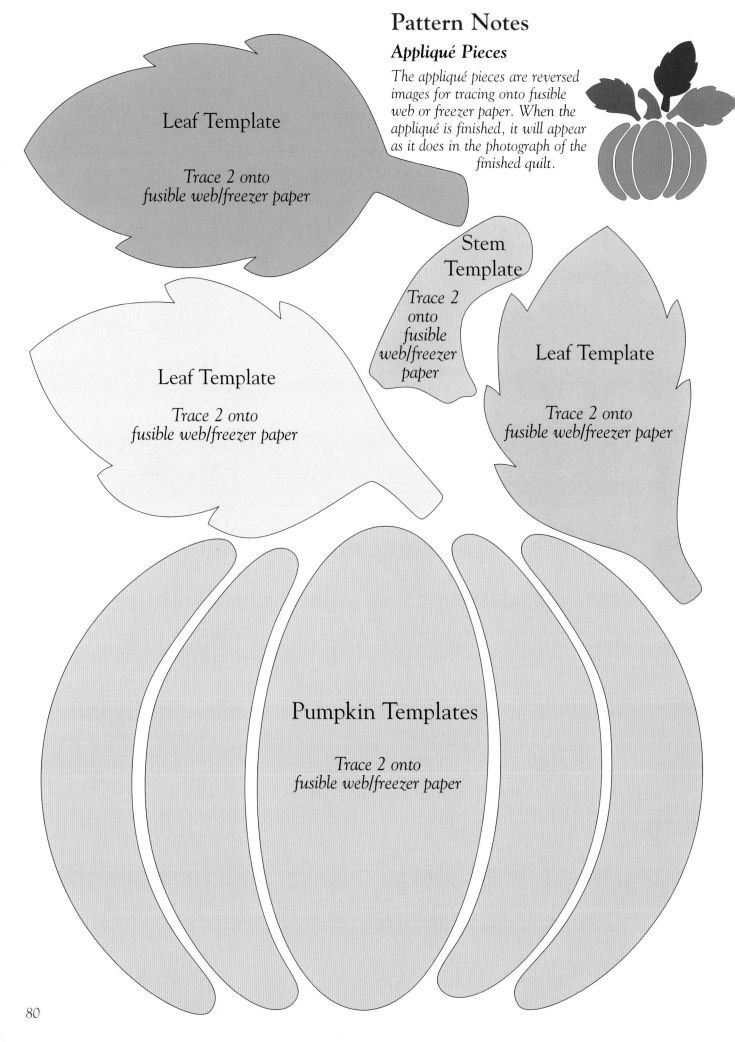

Pattern Notes

Appliqué Pieces

The appliqué pieces are reversed images for tracing onto fusible web or freezer paper. When the appliqué is finished, it will appear as it does in the photograph of the finished quilt.

Leaf Template

Trace 2 onto
fusible web/freezer paper

Stem
Template

Trace 2
onto
*fusible
web/freezer
paper*

Leaf Template

Trace 2 onto
fusible web/freezer paper

Leaf Template

Trace 2 onto
fusible web/freezer paper

Pumpkin Templates

Trace 2 onto
fusible web/freezer paper

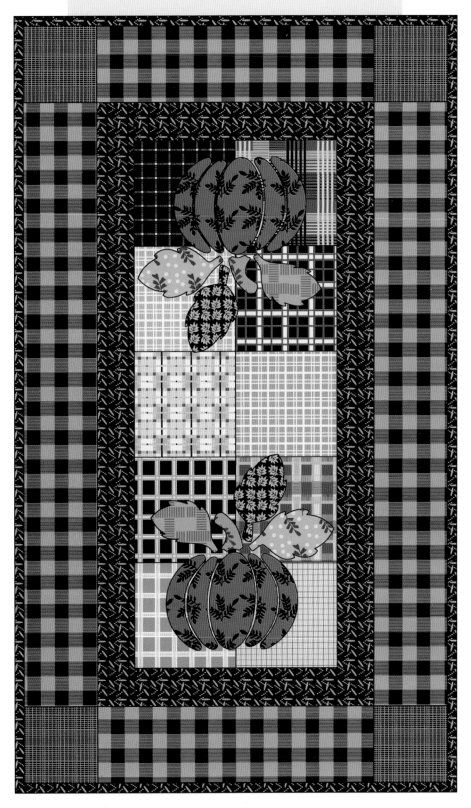

Harvest Pumpkin

Pine Star Runner

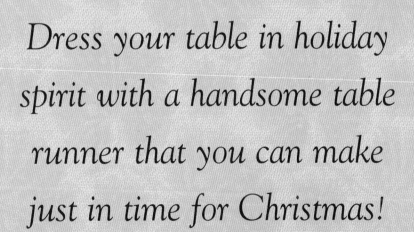

Dress your table in holiday spirit with a handsome table runner that you can make just in time for Christmas!

Pine Star Runner

Table runner measures 23 x 57 inches.
Block measures 12 inches square.

Fabric & Supplies

1/4 yard	**GREEN PRINT #1** for tree points
1/2 yard	**BEIGE PRINT** for background
5/8 yard	**GREEN PRINT #2** for trees and border
1/8 yard	**BROWN PRINT** for tree trunks
3/4 yard	**RED PRINT #1** for star and for side and corner triangles
1/2 yard	**RED PRINT #2** for binding
1-1/2 yards	Backing fabric
Quilt batting	27 x 61 inches

NOTE: read **Getting Started**,
page 216, before beginning this project.

Tree Blocks

Make 2 Blocks

Cutting

From **GREEN PRINT #1** cut
- 1—2-7/8 x 42-inch strip.
- 2—2-1/2-inch squares.

From **BEIGE PRINT** cut
- 2—6-inch squares.
- 1—2-7/8 x 42-inch strip.
- 4—2-1/2-inch squares.

From **GREEN PRINT #2** cut
- 1—4-1/2 x 42-inch strip; from the strip cut 2—4-1/2 x 8-1/2-inch rectangles and 2—4-1/2-inch squares.

From **BROWN PRINT** cut
- 2—1-3/4 x 11-inch strips.

Piecing

1. Layer together the 2-7/8 x 42-inch GREEN PRINT #1 strip and the 2-7/8 x 42-inch BEIGE PRINT strip. Press, but do not sew, the strips together. From the layered strip, crosscut 12, 2-7/8-inch squares.

Crosscut 12—2-7/8-inch squares

2. Cut the layered squares in half diagonally. Stitch 1/4 inch from the diagonal edge of each pair of triangles; press. <u>At this point each triangle-pieced square should measure 2-1/2 inches square.</u>

Make 24—2-1/2-inch triangle-pieced squares

3. Refer to the illustration for placement and sew the Step 2 triangle-pieced squares together in pairs to make 6 of Unit A and 6 of Unit B; press.

Make 6 Unit A   *Make 6 Unit B*

4. Sew a Unit A to both ends of a 4-1/2 x 8-1/2-inch GREEN PRINT #2 rectangle; press. At this point each unit should measure 4-1/2 x 12-1/2 inches.

Make 2

5. Sew a Unit A to the left-hand side of a 4-1/2-inch GREEN PRINT #2 square; press.

Make 2

6. Sew a 2-1/2-inch BEIGE PRINT square to the left-hand side of a Unit B; press. Sew this unit to the bottom of the Step 5 units; press. At this point each unit should measure 6-1/2-inches square.

Make 2

7. Sew the remaining B units together in pairs; press. Sew a 2-1/2-inch GREEN PRINT #1 square to the left-hand side of each unit; press. Sew a 2-1/2-inch BEIGE PRINT square to the right-hand side of each unit; press. Sew these units to the top of the Step 4 units; press. At this point each unit should measure 6-1/2 x 12-1/2 inches.

Make 2

8. Cut the 6-inch BEIGE PRINT squares in half diagonally. Center a BEIGE PRINT triangle on the 1-3/4 x 11-inch BROWN PRINT strip. Stitch a 1/4-inch seam; press the seam allowance toward the BROWN PRINT strip. Center another BEIGE PRINT triangle on the BROWN PRINT strip, stitch and press. The trunk strip will extend beyond the triangles.

Trim the ends of the trunk so that the unit measures 6-1/2 inches square.

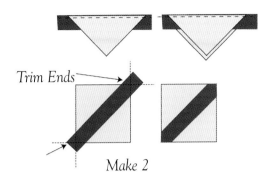

Trim Ends

Make 2

9. Sew the Step 8 trunk units to the right-hand side of the Step 6 units; press.

Make 2

10. Sew the Step 9 units to the bottom of the Step 7 units; press. At this point the blocks should measure 12-1/2 inches square.

Make 2

Star Block

Make 1 Block

Cutting

From **RED PRINT #1** cut
- 1—4-1/2-inch square.
- 8—2-1/2-inch squares.

From **BEIGE PRINT** cut
- 2—2-1/2 x 42-inch strips; from the strips cut
  2—2-1/2 x 12-1/2-inch strips,
  2—2-1/2 x 8-1/2-inch strips,
  4—2-1/2 x 4-1/2-inch rectangles, and
  4—2-1/2-inch squares.

Piecing

1. Position a 2-1/2-inch RED PRINT #1 square on the corner of a 2-1/2 x 4-1/2-inch BEIGE PRINT rectangle. Draw a diagonal line on the RED PRINT #1 square and stitch on the line. Trim away the excess corner fabric, leaving a 1/4-inch seam allowance; press. Repeat this process at the opposite corner of the BEIGE PRINT rectangle. Make 4 units.

Make 4

2. Sew a Step 1 unit to the top and bottom of the 4-1/2-inch RED PRINT #1 square; press. Sew 2-1/2-inch BEIGE PRINT squares to both sides of the remaining Step 1 units; press. Sew these units to the block sides; press. <u>At this point the block should measure 8-1/2 inches square.</u>

Make 1   *Make 1*

3. Sew 2-1/2 x 8-1/2-inch BEIGE PRINT strips to the top and bottom of the Step 2 star block; press. Sew 2-1/2 x 12-1/2-inch BEIGE PRINT strips to the sides of the star block; press. <u>At this point the block should measure 12-1/2 inches square.</u>

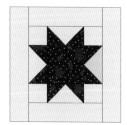

Make 1

Quilt Center

NOTE: The side and corner triangles are cut larger than necessary and will be trimmed before the border is added.

Cutting

From **RED PRINT #1** cut

- 1—19-inch square; cut the square diagonally into quarters for 4 side triangles.
- 2—10-inch squares; cut the squares in half diagonally for 4 corner triangles.

Runner Center Assembly

1. Refer to the quilt illustration and sew together the tree blocks, star block, and side triangles in diagonal rows. Press the seam allowances in alternating directions by rows so the seams will fit snugly together with less bulk.

2. Pin the rows at the block intersections and sew the rows together. Press the seam allowances in one direction.

3. Sew the corner triangles to the runner; press.

4. Trim away the excess fabric from the side and corner triangles, taking care to allow a 1/4-inch seam allowance beyond the corners of each block.

Refer to page 218 for **Trimming Side and Corner Triangles**.

Border

Refer to **Binding and Diagonal Piecing**, page 221 for complete instructions

NOTE: The yardage given allows for the border strips to be cut on the crosswise grain.

Cutting

From **GREEN PRINT #2** cut

- 4—3-1/2 x 42-inch strips for the border.

Attaching the Border

1. Measure the quilt from left to right through the center to determine the length of the top and bottom border strips. Cut 2, 3-1/2-inch wide GREEN PRINT #2 strips to this length, sew them to the top and bottom of the quilt, and press the seams toward the border.

2. Measure the quilt from top to bottom through the center, including the border strips just sewn on, to determine the length of the side borders

strips. Cut 2, 3-1/2-inch wide GREEN PRINT #2 strips to this length, sew them to the sides of the quilt, and press the seams toward the border.

Putting It All Together

Cut the 1-1/2 yard length of backing fabric in half crosswise to make 2, 3/4 yard lengths.

Refer to **Finishing the Quilt** on page 221 for complete instructions.

Binding the Table Runner

Refer to **Binding and Diagonal Piecing** on page 221 for complete instructions with detailed illustrations.

NOTE: The 2-3/4-inch strips will produce a 1/2-inch wide finished double binding. If you would like a wider or narrower binding, adjust the width of the strips.

Cutting

From RED PRINT #2 cut
- 4—2-3/4 x 42-inch strips.

Sew the binding to the quilt using a 3/8-inch seam allowance.

Pine Star Runner

Cottage
THROWS

Discover the joys of creating your own safe haven filled with soul-satisfying comforts. Since simplicity is at the heart of cottage-style decorating, on the pages that follow you'll find nine cozy cottage throws designed to help you surround yourself with the serenity you've been seeking—the essence of country-cottage style!

Midnight Sky

Discover the magic of midnight
with a dramatic quilt filled
with stars and log cabin piecing—
Wide borders accented with
pumpkins and vines
are bound with a bias plaid
binding that brings the color of
the center to the outer edge.

Midnight Sky

Quilt measures 51 x 60 inches.
Block measures 9 inches square.

Fabric & Supplies

3/8 yard	**GOLD PRINT** for stars
5/8 yard	**BLACK PRINT** for star background
1-1/3 yards	**GREEN, GOLD, RED,** and **BROWN PRINTS** for log cabin strips
1/2 yard	**GREEN PRINT** for inner border
1-1/4 yards	**DARK FLORAL** for outer border
5/8 yard	**GREEN PLAID** for binding (cut on bias)
3-1/4 yards	Backing fabric
Quilt batting	55 x 64 inches

Optional Appliqué

1/4 yard	**ORANGE PRINT** for pumpkins
1/2 yard	**GREEN PRINT #1** for leaves
5 x 12 inches	**GREEN PRINT #2** for pumpkin stems
1/2 yard	**GREEN PRINT #3** for vines
3-inch squares	**ASSORTED FABRICS** (24 squares) for berry appliqués

Freezer paper for pumpkin, leaf, stem, and berry appliqués

#8 Green and variegated gold pearl cotton for appliqué

NOTE: *read* **Getting Started,**
page 216, before beginning this project.

Star Blocks

Make 20 Blocks

Cutting

From **GOLD PRINT** cut
- 5—2 x 42-inch strips; from the strips cut 40—2-inch squares and 20—2 x 5-inch rectangles.

From **BLACK PRINT** cut
- 8—2 x 42-inch strips; from the strips cut 80—2-inch squares and 40—2 x 3-1/2-inch rectangles.

Piecing

1. Position 2, 2-inch BLACK PRINT squares on the corners of the 2 x 5-inch GOLD PRINT rectangles. Draw a diagonal line on the BLACK PRINT squares and stitch on this line. Trim the seam allowances to 1/4 inch; press.

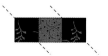 *Make 20*

2. Position a 2-inch GOLD PRINT square on the corner of each 2 x 3-1/2-inch BLACK PRINT rectangle. Draw a diagonal line on the GOLD PRINT squares and stitch on the line. Trim the seam allowance to 1/4 inch; press. Add a 2-inch BLACK PRINT square to each unit, as shown.

 Make 40

3. Sew the Step 2 units to the top and bottom of the Step 1 units; press. <u>At this point each star block should measure 5 inches square.</u>

 Make 20

Log Cabin Strips

Cutting

From **GREEN, GOLD, RED,** and **BROWN PRINTS** cut
- 20—2 x 42-inch strips.

Piecing

NOTE: Add the strips to the star blocks in a random fashion so the fabrics appear in different positions in each block. The strips will be cut after they are sewn to the block.

1. Referring to the illustration, sew a 2 x 42-inch strip to the star block. Press the seam allowance toward the strip and trim away the excess fabric.

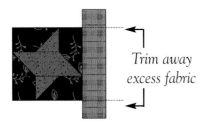

Trim away excess fabric

2. Turn the block a quarter turn to the right. Sew the next strip to the block, as shown. Press the seam allowance toward the strip and trim away the excess fabric.

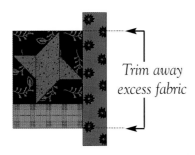

Trim away excess fabric

3. Referring to the illustration, continue adding strips to the block in the same fashion, making sure strips are only added to two sides of each block. Press and trim away the excess fabric from each strip as it is sewn to the block. <u>When a total of six strips have been added, block should measure 9-1/2 inches square.</u>

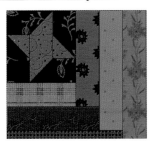

Make 20

Quilt Center

Quilt Center Assembly

1. Referring to the illustration, lay out the blocks. Rotate the blocks so that the stars alternate positions from row to row.

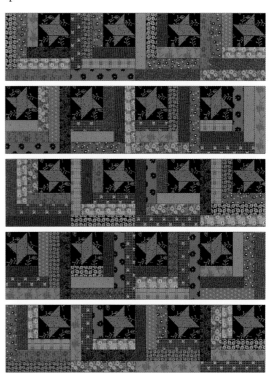

2. Sew the blocks together in 5 horizontal rows of 4 blocks each. Press the seams in alternating directions by rows so the seams will fit snugly together with less bulk. Sew the rows together; press.

Borders

Refer to **Binding and Diagonal Piecing** on page 221 for complete instructions with detailed illustrations.

NOTE: The yardage given allows for the border strips to be cut on the crosswise grain. Diagonally piece the strips as needed.

Cutting

From **GREEN PRINT** cut
- 5—2 x 42-inch strips for the inner border.

From **DARK FLORAL** cut
- 6—6 x 42-inch strips for the outer border.

Attaching the Borders

1. Measure the quilt from left to right through the center to determine the length of the top and

bottom inner border strips. Cut 2, 2-inch wide GREEN PRINT strips to this measurement, sew them to the top and bottom of the quilt, and press the seams toward the border.

2. Measure the quilt from top to bottom through the center to determine the length of the side inner border strips. Cut 2, 2-inch wide GREEN PRINT strips to this measurement, sew them to the sides of the quilt, and press the seams toward the border.

3. For the top and bottom outer border strips, measure the quilt as in Step 1. Cut 2, 6-inch wide DARK FLORAL strips to this measurement, sew them to the top and bottom of the quilt, and press seams toward the border.

4. For the side outer border strips, measure the quilt as in Step 2. Cut 2, 6-inch wide DARK FLORAL strips to the measurement, sew them to the sides of the quilt, and press the seams toward the border.

Appliqué

Cutting

From GREEN PRINT #3 cut
- 1-3/8-inch wide bias strips to make a 150-inch long strip for the vines.

Diagonally piece the strips together.

Refer to **Binding and Diagonal Piecing** on page 221 for complete instructions with detailed illustrations.

Fold and Press Method

Prepare the Vines

1. Fold the GREEN PRINT #3 strip in half lengthwise, with wrong sides together; press. Fold the strip in half again so the raw edges are hidden by the first folded edge; press.

2. Cut the GREEN PRINT #3 strip into the following segments:
   - 1—36-inch long strip
   - 3—33-inch long strips
   - 2—6-inch long strips.

3. Lay the quilt top on a flat surface for pinning and basting the vines in place. Refer to the quilt illustration for positioning the strips; pin and baste the vines in place. Using matching thread, appliqué the vines.

Freezer Paper Method

Prepare the Pumpkins, Leaves, Stems, and Berries

Use this method of hand-appliqué for a traditional finished look. The freezer paper forms a base around which the fabric is shaped.

1. Lay the freezer paper, paper side up, on the appliqué shapes. Trace the shapes and cut out along the traced lines.

2. With a dry iron on wool setting, press the coated side of the freezer-paper shapes to the wrong side of the fabrics, allowing 3/4 inch between each shape. Cut out the shapes 1/4 inch beyond the edge of the freezer paper and finger-press the edge of the fabric over the edge of the freezer paper.

3. Position and pin the appliqué shapes to the patchwork center, referring to the quilt illustration and photograph. Use matching thread and small slip stitches to appliqué the shape by needle-turning the seam allowance under the edge of the freezer paper. When there is about 3/4 inch remaining to appliqué on each shape, slide the needle into the opening and use it to loosen the freezer paper. Gently remove the paper and finish stitching the shape in place.

4. Appliqué the remaining shapes to the quilt.

5. Mark the veins on the leaves and the sections on the pumpkins, referring to the pattern pieces. Using 1 strand of #8 green pearl cotton, stem stitch the vein details on the leaves. Using 1 strand of variegated #8 gold pearl cotton, stem stitch the section details on the pumpkins.

Putting It All Together

Cut the 3-1/4 yard length of backing fabric in half crosswise to make 2, 1-5/8 yard lengths.

Refer to **Finishing the Quilt** on page 221 for complete instructions.

Binding the Quilt

Refer to **Binding and Diagonal Piecing** on page 221 for complete instructions with detailed illustrations.

NOTE: *The 2-3/4-inch strips will produce a 1/2-inch wide finished double binding. If you would like a wider or narrower binding, adjust the width of the strips.*

Cutting for Bias Binding

From **GREEN PLAID** cut

• 2-3/4-inch wide bias strips to make a strip approximately 230 inches long.

Sew the binding to the quilt using a 3/8-inch seam allowance.

Pattern Notes

Appliqué Pieces

The appliqué pieces are reversed images for tracing onto freezer paper. When the appliqué is finished, it will appear as it does in the photograph of the finished quilt.

Leaf Template

Trace 4 onto freezer paper

Leaf Template

Trace 4 as shown and 6 reversed onto freezer paper

Pattern Notes

Appliqué Pieces

The appliqué pieces are reversed images for tracing onto freezer paper. When the appliqué is finished, it will appear as it does in the photograph of the finished quilt.

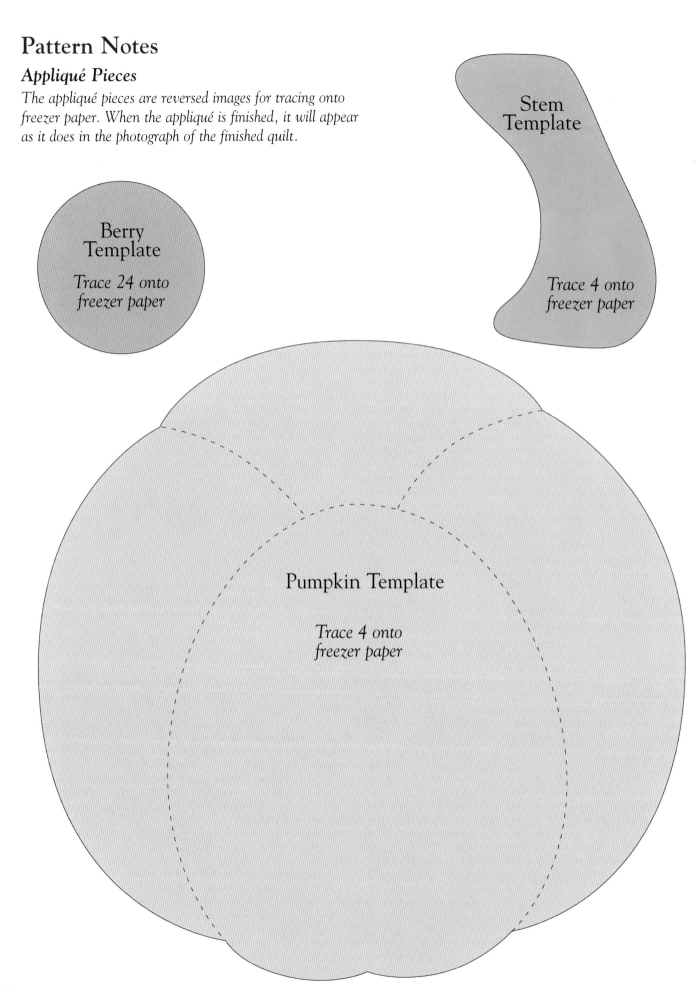

Stem
Template

Trace 4 onto
freezer paper

Berry
Template

Trace 24 onto
freezer paper

Pumpkin Template

Trace 4 onto
freezer paper

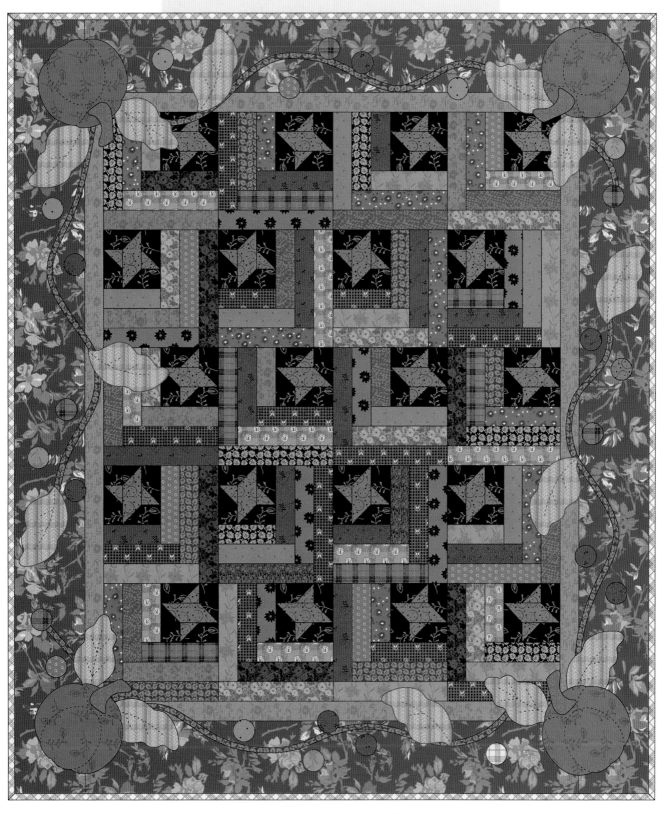

Midnight Sky

Harvest Patches

For stunning results,
small touches of repeated
color provide greater
impact for a collection of
multi-colored prints
that combine simple shapes
into one unified block.

Harvest Patches

Quilt measures 52 x 64 inches.
Block measures 10 inches square.

Fabric & Supplies

1/4 yard	**RED PRINT #1** for blocks	
5/8 yard	**GREEN PRINT #1** for blocks	
1/2 yard	**BLACK PRINT** for blocks	
1/4 yard	**BLACK LARGE FLORAL** for center square in blocks	
3/4 yard	**TAN PRINT** for blocks	
1 yard	**GREEN PRINT #2** for lattice and middle border	
1/4 yard	**RED PRINT #2** for lattice posts	
1-1/3 yard	**BEIGE BERRY/LEAF PRINT** for inner and outer borders	
5/8 yard	**GREEN PRINT #2** for binding	
3-1/4 yards	Backing fabric	
Quilt batting	56 x 68 inches	

NOTE: read **Getting Started**,
page 216, before beginning this project.

Blocks

Make 12 Blocks

Cutting

From **RED PRINT #1** cut
- 4—1-1/2 x 42-inch strips.

From **GREEN PRINT #1** cut
- 4—2-1/2 x 42-inch strips.
- 4—1-1/2 x 42-inch strips.

From **BLACK PRINT** cut
- 2—3-1/2 x 42-inch strips.
- 2—2-1/2 x 42-inch strips.

From **BLACK LARGE FLORAL** cut
- 1—3-1/2 x 42-inch strip; from the strip cut 12—3-1/2-inch squares.

From **TAN PRINT** cut
- 3—4-1/2 x 42-inch strips; from the strips cut 24—4-1/2-inch squares. Cut the squares diagonally into quarters, forming 96 side triangles.
- 2—3-1/2 x 42-inch strips; from the strips cut 24—3-1/2-inch squares. Cut the squares diagonally in half, forming 48 corner triangles.

NOTE: The blocks are made up of strip sets.
Refer to page 220 for **Hints and Helps for Pressing Strip Sets**.

Piecing

1. Aligning long edges, sew together a 1-1/2-inch wide RED PRINT #1 strip, a 1-1/2-inch wide GREEN #1 PRINT strip, and a 2-1/2-inch wide BLACK PRINT strip; press. Make 2 strip sets. Cut the strip sets into segments.

Strip Set A
Crosscut 24, 3-1/2-inch wide segments

2. Aligning long edges, sew a 2-1/2-inch wide GREEN PRINT #1 strip to both sides of a 3-12-inch wide BLACK PRINT strip; press. Make 2 strip sets. Cut the strip sets into segments.

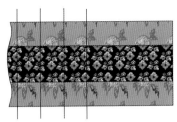

Strip Set B
Crosscut 24, 2-1/2-inch wide segments

3. Aligning long edges, sew together a 1-1/2-inch wide RED PRINT #1 strip and a 1-1/2-inch wide GREEN PRINT #1 strip; press. Make 2 strip sets. Cut the strip sets into segments.

Strip Set C
Crosscut 24, 3-1/2-inch wide segments

4. Sew a Strip Set A segment to both sides of a 3-1/2-inch BLACK LARGE FLORAL square; press. Add TAN PRINT corner triangles to both ends of the unit; press.

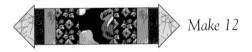 *Make 12*

5. Sew TAN PRINT side triangles to both ends of a Strip Set B segment; press.

 *Make 24*

6. Sew TAN PRINT side triangles to both ends of a Strip Set C segment; press.

 *Make 24*

7. Referring to the block assembly illustration, sew the Step 4, 5, and 6 units together in diagonal rows; press. Add the 2 remaining TAN PRINT corner triangles. Trim away the excess fabric from

the side and corner triangles, taking care to allow a 1/4-inch seam allowance beyond the corner points of the RED PRINT #1 and GREEN PRINT #1 pieces. <u>At this point each block should measure 10-1/2 inches square.</u>

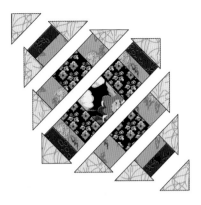

 *Make 12*

Refer to page 218 for **Trimming Side and Corner Triangles**.

Quilt Center

Cutting

From **GREEN PRINT #2** cut
- 8—2-1/2 x 42-inch strips; from the strips cut 31—2-1/2 x 10-1/2-inch lattice strips.

From **RED PRINT #2** cut
- 2—2-1/2 x 42-inch strips; from the strips cut 20—2-1/2-inch squares for lattice posts.

Quilt Center Assembly

1. Referring to the illustration, sew together 3, 2-1/2 x 10-1/2-inch GREEN PRINT #2 lattice strips and 4, 2-1/2-inch RED PRINT #2 lattice posts; press.

Make 5

2. Referring to the illustration, sew together 3 pieced blocks and 4, 2-1/2 x 10-1/2-inch GREEN PRINT #2 lattice strips; press.

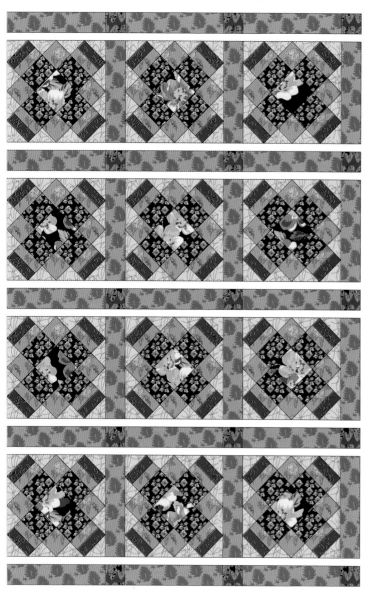

Make 4 block rows

3. Referring to the quilt illustration, pin the block rows and lattice strips together at the block intersections. Sew the block rows and lattice strips together; press. <u>At this point the quilt center should measure 38-1/2 x 50-1/2 inches.</u>

Borders

Refer to **Binding and Diagonal Piecing** on page 221 for complete instructions with detailed illustrations.

NOTE: The yardage given allows for the border strips to be cut on the crosswise grain.

Cutting

From **BEIGE BERRY/LEAF PRINT** cut
- 6—3-1/2 x 42-inch strips for the inner border.
- 6—3-1/2 x 42-inch strips for the outer border.

From **GREEN PRINT #2** cut
- 5—1-1/2 x 42-inch strips for the middle border.

Attaching the Borders

1. Measure the quilt from left to right through the center to determine the length of the top and bottom inner border strips. Cut 2, 3-1/2-inch wide BEIGE BERRY/LEAF PRINT strips to this measurement and pin them to the top and bottom of the quilt. Sew the strips to the quilt and press the seam allowances toward the border.

2. Measure the quilt from the top to bottom through the center, including the border strips just added, to determine the length of the side inner border strips. Cut 2, 3-1/2-inch wide BEIGE BERRY/LEAF PRINT strips to this measurement and pin them to the sides of the quilt. Sew the strips to the quilt and press the seam allowances toward the border.

3. Measure the quilt from left to right through the center to determine the length of the top and bottom middle border strips. Cut 2, 1-1/2-inch wide GREEN PRINT #2 strips to this measurement and pin them to the top and bottom of the quilt. Sew the strips to the quilt and press the seam allowances toward the border.

4. Measure the quilt from the top to bottom through the center, including the border strips just added, to determine the length of the side middle border strips. Cut 2, 1-1/2-inch wide GREEN PRINT #2 strips to this measurement and pin them to the sides of the quilt. Sew the strips to the quilt and press the seam allowances toward the border.

5. Measure the quilt from left to right through the center to determine the length of the top and bottom outer border strips. Cut 2, 3-1/2-inch wide BEIGE BERRY/LEAF PRINT strips to this measurement and pin them to the top and

bottom of the quilt. Sew the strips to the quilt and press the seam allowances toward the border.

6. Measure the quilt from top to bottom through the center, including the border strips just added to determine the length of the side outer border strips. Cut 2, 3-1/2-inch wide BEIGE BERRY/LEAF PRINT strips to this measurement and pin them to the sides of the quilt. Sew the strips to the quilt and press the seam allowances toward the border.

Putting It All Together

Cut the 3-1/4-yard length of backing fabric in half crosswise to make 2, 1-5/8-yard lengths.

Refer to **Finishing the Quilt** on page 221 for complete instructions.

Binding the Quilt

Refer to **Binding and Diagonal Piecing** on page 221 for complete instructions with detailed illustrations.

NOTE: The 2-3/4-inch strips will produce a 1/2-inch wide finished double binding. If you would like a wider or narrower binding, adjust the width of the strips you cut.

Cutting

From **GREEN PRINT #2** cut
- 6—2-3/4 x 42-inch strips.

Sew the binding to the quilt using a 3/8-inch seam allowance.

Harvest Patches

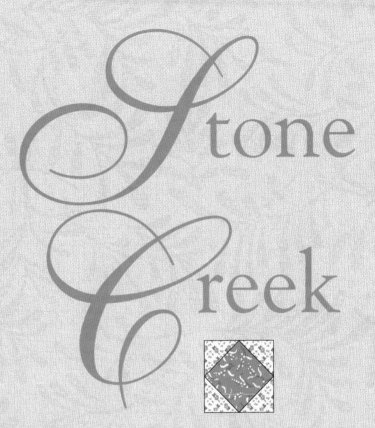

Stone Creek

Center blocks in soft, subtle
shades of spring are framed
by an interesting border—
wide enough that the quilt
can easily serve as a
traditional bed quilt.

Stone Creek

Quilt measures 80 x 96 inches.
Block measures 8 inches square.

Fabric & Supplies

1-1/2 yards	**ROSE VINE PRINT** for Block A and small corner squares
1-1/4 yards	**BEIGE PRINT #1** for Block A
2 yards	**GREEN PRINT** for Block B and outer border strip
2-1/4 yards	**BEIGE FLORAL** for Block B and outer border strip
3/4 yard	**ROSE PRINT** for Block C and large corner squares
1/2 yard	**GREEN FLORAL** for Block C
1-1/2 yards	**BEIGE PRINT #2** for Block C and outer border strip
1-1/4 yards	**DARK GREEN-ON-GREEN-PLAID** for Block C and outer border strip
1-1/4 yards	**SMALL GREEN PLAID** for inner border
1 yard	**SMALL GREEN PLAID** for binding (cut on bias)
5-3/4 yards	Backing Fabric
Quilt batting	84 x 100-inches

NOTE: read **Getting Started**,
page 216, before beginning this project.

Block A

Make 18 Blocks

Cutting

From **ROSE VINE PRINT** cut
- 5—8-1/2 x 42-inch strips; from the strips cut 18—8-1/2-inch squares.

From **BEIGE PRINT #1** cut
- 9—4-1/2 x 42-inch strips; from the strips cut 72—4-1/2-inch squares.

Piecing

1. Position a 4-1/2-inch BEIGE PRINT #1 square on the corner of an 8-1/2-inch ROSE VINE PRINT square. Draw a diagonal line on BEIGE PRINT #1 square, and stitch on the line. Trim the seam allowance to 1/4 inch; press. Repeat this process at the opposite corner of the ROSE VINE PRINT square.

2. Repeat Step 1 positioning BEIGE PRINT #1 squares on opposite corners of the ROSE VINE PRINT square. <u>At this point each block should measure 8-1/2 inches square.</u>

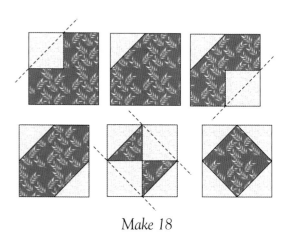

Make 18

Block B

Make 21 Blocks

From **GREEN PRINT** cut
- 6—8-1/2 x 42-inch strips; from the strips cut 21—8-1/2-inch squares.

From **BEIGE FLORAL** cut
- 10—4-1/2 x 42-inch strips; from the strips cut 84—4-1/2-inch squares.

Using 4-1/2-inch BEIGE FLORAL squares and 8-1/2-inch GREEN PRINT squares, follow instructions in Steps 1 and 2 for Block A. <u>At this point each block should measure 8-1/2 inches square.</u>

Make 21

Block C

Make 24 Blocks

Cutting

From **ROSE PRINT** cut
- 2—6-5/8 x 42-inch strips.

From **GREEN FLORAL** cut
- 2—6-5/8 x 42-inch strips.

From **BEIGE PRINT #2** cut
- 4—5-1/4 x 42-inch strips; from the strips cut 24—5-1/4-inch squares. Cut the squares diagonally into quarters to make 96 triangles.

From **DARK GREEN-ON-GREEN PLAID** cut
- 4—5-1/4 x 42-inch strips; from the strips cut 24—5-1/4-inch squares. Cut the squares diagonally into quarters to make 96 triangles.

Piecing

1. With right sides together, layer the 6-5/8 x 42-inch ROSE PRINT and GREEN FLORAL strips in pairs. Press together, but do not sew. Cut the layered strips into 6-5/8-inch squares.

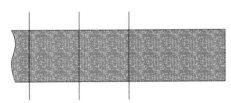

Crosscut 12, 6-5/8-inch squares

2. Cut the layered squares in half diagonally to make 24 sets of triangles. Stitch 1/4 inch from the diagonal edge of each pair of triangles; press. <u>At this point each triangle-pieced square should measure 6-1/4 inches square.</u>

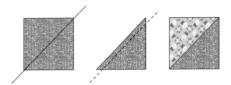

Make 24, 6-1/4-inch triangle-pieced squares

3. With right sides together, layer a BEIGE PRINT #2 triangle and a DARK GREEN-ON-GREEN PLAID triangle. Stitch along the bias edge as shown, being careful not to stretch the triangles; press. Repeat for the remaining BEIGE PRINT #2 and DARK GREEN-ON-GREEN PLAID triangles. Make sure you sew with the DARK GREEN-ON-GREEN PLAID triangle on top, and sew along the same bias edge of each triangle set so that the pieced triangle units will all have the DARK GREEN-ON-GREEN PLAID triangle on the same side.

Bias edges

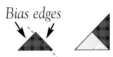

Make 96 identical triangle-pieced units

4. Accurately center Step 3 BEIGE/DARK GREEN-ON-GREEN PLAID triangle units on 2 opposite sides of a Step 2 triangle-pieced square. Sew the pieces together; press the seam allowances toward the triangle-pieced square.

Make 24

5. Repeat Step 3 centering Step 3 BEIGE/DARK GREEN-ON-GREEN PLAID triangle units on the remaining opposite sides of the triangle-pieced square. Sew the pieces together; press. <u>At this point each block should measure 8-1/2 inches square.</u>

Make 24

Quilt Center

1. Referring to the quilt illustration for block placement, sew the A, B, and C blocks together in 9 horizontal rows of 7 blocks each. Press the seam allowances in alternating directions by rows so the seams will fit snugly together with less bulk.

Sew together 9 rows of 7 blocks

2. Pin the rows at the block intersections; sew the rows together. Press the seam allowances in one direction. <u>At this point the quilt center should measure 56-1/2 x 72-1/2 inches.</u>

Borders

Refer to **Binding and Diagonal Piecing** on page 221 for complete instructions with detailed illustrations.

NOTE: The yardage given allows for the border strips to be cut on the crosswise grain. Diagonally piece the strips as needed.

Cutting

From **SMALL GREEN PLAID** cut
• 8—4-1/2 x 42-inch strips for inner border.

From **ROSE VINE PRINT** cut
• 4—4-1/2-inch small corner squares.

From **DARK GREEN-ON-GREEN PLAID** and **GREEN PRINT** cut
• 2—8-1/2 x 42-inch strips from each for outer border.

From **BEIGE FLORAL** and **BEIGE PRINT #2** cut
• 3—8-1/2 x 42-inch strips from each for outer border.

From **ROSE PRINT** cut
• 4—8-1/2-inch large corner squares.

Attaching the Borders

1. Measure the quilt from left to right through the center to determine the length of the top and bottom inner border strips. Cut 2, 4-1/2-inch wide SMALL GREEN PLAID strips to this measurement and pin them to the top and bottom of the quilt. Sew the strips to the quilt and press the seam allowances toward the border.

2. Measure the quilt from the top to bottom through the center, including the seam allowances but not the border strips just added, to determine the length of the side inner border strips. Cut 2, 4-1/2-inch wide SMALL GREEN PLAID strips to this measurement and sew a 4-1/2-inch ROSE VINE PRINT small corner square to each end; press. Pin and sew the strips to the quilt and press the seam allowances toward the border.

3. Measure the quilt from left to right through the center to determine the length of the top and bottom outer border strips. Cut 1, 8-1/2-inch wide DARK GREEN-ON-GREEN PLAID strip and 1, 8-1/2-inch wide GREEN PRINT strip to this measurement and pin them to the top and bottom of the quilt. Sew the strips to the quilt and press the seam allowances toward the border.

4. Measure the quilt from the top to bottom through the center, including the seam

allowances but not the border strips just added, to determine the length of the side outer border strips. Cut 1, 8-1/2-inch wide BEIGE FLORAL strip and 1, 8-1/2-inch wide BEIGE PRINT #2 strip to this measurement and sew an 8-1/2-inch ROSE PRINT larger corner square to each end; press. Pin and sew the strips to the quilt and press the seam allowances toward the border.

Putting It All Together

Cut the 5-3/4 yard length of backing fabric in half crosswise to make 2, 2-7/8 yard lengths.

Refer to **Finishing the Quilt** on page 221 for complete instructions.

Binding the Quilt

Refer to **Binding and Diagonal Piecing** on page 221 for complete instructions with detailed illustrations.

NOTE: The 2-3/4-inch strips will produce a 1/2-inch wide finished double binding. If you would like a wider or narrower binding, adjust the width of the strips you cut.

Cutting for Bias Binding

From **SMALL GREEN PLAID** cut
- 2-3/4-inch wide bias strips to make a strip approximately 370-inches long.

Sew the binding to the quilt using a 3/8-inch seam allowance.

Stone Creek

Sunporch
Basket

An antique block carefully
saved from a 60-year-old
quilt is the inspiration
for the flower-filled
basket appliqués on this
charming cottage quilt.

Sunporch Basket

Quilt measures 68 x 84 inches.
Block measures 11-1/2 inches square.

Fabric & Supplies

2-3/8 yards	**BEIGE PRINT** for foundation squares and borders
1 yard	**GREEN GRID** for basket appliqués
1/4 yard	**BLUE PLAID** for flower appliqués
1/4 yard	**ROSE PLAID** for flower appliqués
1/4 yard	**GOLD PRINT** for flower appliqués
1/4 yard	**GREEN PRINT** for flower appliqués
3-7/8 yards	**BLUE FLORAL** for alternate blocks, side and corner triangles, and borders
1 yard	**GOLD PLAID** for binding (cut on bias)
5 yards	Backing fabric
Quilt batting	72 x 88 inches
2 yards	Freezer paper for appliqué

#8 Pearl cotton or embroidery floss in matching colors or contrasting colors for decorative stitches

NOTE: read **Getting Started**, page 216, before beginning this project.

Basket Blocks

Make 12 Blocks

Cutting

From **BEIGE PRINT** cut
- 4—12 x 42-inch strips; from the strips cut 12—12-inch appliqué foundation squares.

From **GREEN GRID** cut
- 6—3 x 42-inch strips; from the strips cut 12—3 x 17-inch strips for basket handle appliqués.

NOTE: *Make a template of the basket unit to use as a Basket Placement Guide. To do so, photocopy the basket unit on page 114, glue the paper to a manila folder to stabilize it, and cut out the shape. Use the outer portion for the Basket Placement Guide template and discard the inner portion.*

Basket Handle Appliqué

1. Fold a 3 x 17-inch GREEN GRID strip in half lengthwise, with wrong sides together; press. To keep the raw edges aligned, stitch 1/4 inch away from the raw edges. Fold the strip in half again so the raw edges are hidden by the first folded edge; press.

2. Position the Placement Guide on point on a 12-inch BEIGE PRINT appliqué foundation square. Lay the prepared basket handle inside this shape for placement. Pin the handle in place, remove the Placement Guide, and with matching thread, hand-stitch the handle in place. Make 12.

Freezer Paper Method

Basket, Flower, and Leaf Appliqués

With this method of hand appliqué, the freezer paper forms a base around which the basket, flower, and leaf appliqués are shaped.

1. Lay the freezer paper, paper side up, on the appliqué shapes. Trace the shapes and cut out along the traced lines.

2. With a dry iron on wool setting, press the coated side of the freezer paper shapes to the wrong side of the fabrics, allowing at least 3/4 inch between each shape.

3. Cut out the shapes 1/4 inch beyond the edge of the freezer paper and finger-press the edge of the fabric over the edge of the freezer paper.

4. Again, position the Basket Placement Guide on a BEIGE PRINT appliqué foundation square. Lay the prepared basket inside this shape for placement. Pin the basket in place, remove the Placement Guide, and with matching thread, handstitch the basket in place. When there is about 3/4 inch left to appliqué on the basket, slide your needle into this opening and loosen the freezer paper. Gently remove it, and finish stitching the basket in place.

5. Referring to the quilt illustration, position the leaves on the block and pin in place. With matching thread, hand-stitch the leaves. Remove the freezer paper as described in Step 4.

6. Referring to the quilt illustration, position the flowers on the block and pin in place. With matching thread, hand-stitch the flowers. Remove the freezer paper as described in Step 4.

7. Using #8 pearl cotton, button-hole-stitch around the edges of the leaves and flowers.

8. Using #8 pearl cotton, stem-stitch the lines in each flower center.

Quilt Center

NOTE: The side and corner triangles are larger than necessary and will be trimmed before the borders are added.

Cutting

From **BLUE FLORAL** cut
- 2—12x 42-inch strips; from the strips cut 6—12-inch alternate block squares.
- 2—18 x 42-inch strips; from the strips cut 3—18-inch squares. Cut the squares diagonally into quarters for a total of 12 triangles. You will be using 10 for the side triangles. 2—10-inch squares. Cut the squares in half diagonally for a total of 4 corner triangles.

Quilt Center Assembly

1. Referring to the quilt illustration for block placement, sew the appliquéd basket blocks, alternating blocks, and side triangles together in

diagonal rows. Press the seam allowances toward the BLUE FLORAL alternate blocks so the seams will fit snugly together with less bulk.

2. Pin the rows at the block intersections, and sew the rows together. Press the seam allowances in one direction.

3. Sew the corner triangles to the quilt center; press.

4. Trim away the excess fabric from the side and corner triangles, taking care to allow a 1/4-inch seam allowance beyond the corners of each block.

Refer to page 218 for **Trimming Side and Corner Triangles**.

Borders

Refer to **Binding and Diagonal Piecing** on page 221 for complete instructions with detailed illustrations.

NOTE: The yardage given allows for the border strips to be cut on the crosswise grain.

Cutting

From **BEIGE PRINT** cut
- 6—2-1/2 x 42-inch inner border strips.
- 7—1-1/2 x 42-inch middle border strips.

From **BLUE FLORAL** cut
- 7—1-1/2 x 42-inch middle border strips.
- 9—6-1/2 x 42-inch outer border strips.

Attaching the Borders

1. Measure the quilt from left to right through the center to determine the length of the top and bottom inner border strips. Cut 2, 2-1/2-inch wide BEIGE PRINT strips to this measurement and pin them to the top and bottom of the quilt. Sew the strips to the quilt and press the seam allowances toward the border.

2. Measure the quilt from the top to bottom through the center, including the border strips just added, to determine the length of the side inner border strips. Cut 2, 2-1/2-inch wide BEIGE PRINT strips to this measurement and pin them to the top and bottom of the quilt. Sew the strips to the quilt and press the seam allowances toward the border.

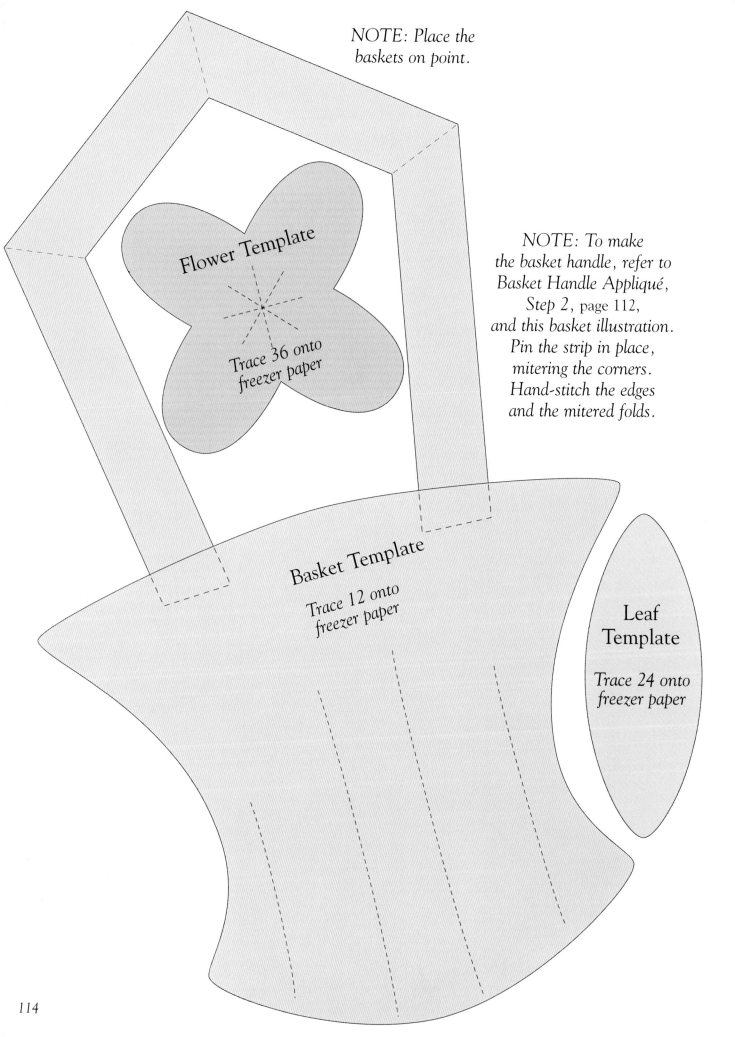

NOTE: Place the
baskets on point.

Flower Template

Trace 36 onto
freezer paper

NOTE: To make
the basket handle, refer to
Basket Handle Appliqué,
Step 2, page 112,
and this basket illustration.
Pin the strip in place,
mitering the corners.
Hand-stitch the edges
and the mitered folds.

Basket Template

Trace 12 onto
freezer paper

Leaf
Template

Trace 24 onto
freezer paper

3. Measure the quilt from left to right through the center to determine the length of the top and bottom middle border strips. Cut 2, 1-1/2-inch wide BLUE FLORAL strips to this measurement and pin them to the top and bottom of the quilt. Sew the strips to the quilt and press the seam allowances toward the border.

4. Measure the quilt from top to bottom through the center, including the border strips just added, to determine the length of the top and bottom middle border strips. Cut 2, 1-1/2-inch wide BLUE FLORAL strips to this measurement and pin them to the sides of the quilt. Sew the strips to the quilt and press the seam allowances toward the border.

5. Measure the quilt from left to right through the center to determine the length of the top and bottom middle border strips. Cut 2, 1-1/2-inch wide BEIGE PRINT strips to this measurement and pin them to the top and bottom of the quilt. Sew the strips to the quilt and press the seam allowances toward the border.

6. Measure the quilt from the top to bottom through the center, including the border strips just added, to determine the length of the side middle border strips. Cut 2, 1-1/2-inch wide BEIGE PRINT strips to this measurement and pin them to the sides of the quilt. Sew the strips to the quilt and press the seam allowances toward the border. Trim excess fabric from the ends of the border strips.

7. Measure the quilt from left to right through the center to determine the length of the top and bottom outer border strips. Cut 2, 6-1/2-inch wide BLUE FLORAL strips to this measurement and pin them to the top and bottom of the quilt. Sew the strips to the quilt and press the seam allowances toward the border.

8. Measure the quilt from the top to bottom through the center, including the border strips just added, to determine the length of the side outer border strips. Cut 2, 6-1/2-inch wide BLUE FLORAL strips to this measurement and pin them to the sides of the quilt. Sew the strips to the quilt and press the seam allowances toward the border. Trim excess fabric from the ends of the border strips.

Putting It All Together

Cut the 5-yard length of backing fabric in half crosswise to make 2, 2-1/2-yard lengths.

Refer to **Finishing the Quilt** on page 221 for complete instructions.

Binding the Quilt

Cutting

Refer to **Binding and Diagonal Piecing** on page 221 for complete instructions with detailed illustrations.

NOTE: *The 2-3/4-inch strips will produce a 1/2-inch wide finished double binding. If you would like a wider or narrower binding, adjust the width of the strips.*

From **GOLD PLAID** cut
- 2-3/4-inch wide bias strips to make a strip approximately 350-inches long.

Sew the binding to the quilt using a 3/8-inch seam allowance.

Sunporch Basket

Tall Houses

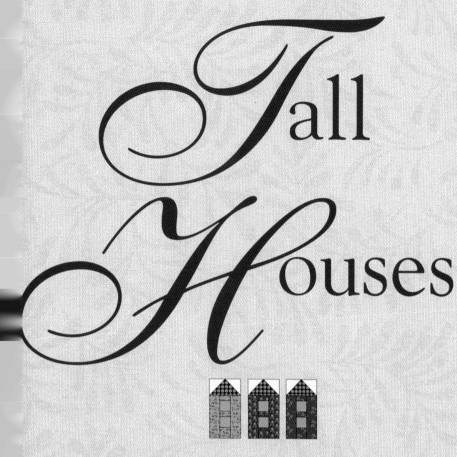

Tall houses work up in
short order on this fast
and fun scrap quilt.
The over-sized motifs
which include lattice
stars are ideal for flannels,
calicos, or a
combination of both.

Tall Houses

Quilt measures 57-1/2 x 80 inches.
Block measures 9 x 16-1/2 inches.

If using flannel, refer to **Helpful Hints**
for Sewing with Flannel *on page 219.*

Fabric & Supplies

1/4 yard	**9 COORDINATING FABRICS** for house blocks
1/4 yard	**GOLD PRINT** for windows
1/2 yard	**BLACK PRINT** for roofs
1 yard	**BEIGE PRINT** for block background
3/4 yard	**CHESTNUT PRINT** for stars
1 yard	**TAN PRINT** for lattice
3/4 yard	**DARK GREEN PRINT** for middle border and corner squares
2 yards	**TAN LEAF PRINT** for outer border (cut lengthwise)
3/4 yard	**CHESTNUT PRINT** for binding
3-3/4 yards	Backing fabric
Quilt batting	62 x 84 inches

NOTE: *read* **Getting Started**,
page 216, before beginning this project.

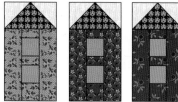

House Blocks

Make 9 Blocks

Cutting

From each of the **9 COORDINATING FABRICS** cut
- 1—3-1/2 x 42-inch strip; from the strip cut 2—3-1/2 x 12-1/2-inch rectangles, 2—2 x 3-1/2-inch rectangles, and 1—3-1/2-inch square.

From **GOLD PRINT** cut
- 2—3-1/2 x 42-inch strips; from the strips cut 18—3-1/2-inch squares.

From **BLACK PRINT** cut
- 3—5 x 42-inch strips; from the strips cut 9—5 x 9-1/2-inch rectangles.

From **BEIGE PRINT** cut
- 3—5 x 42-inch strips; from the strips cut 18—5-inch squares.

Piecing

1. With right sides together, position a 5-inch BEIGE PRINT square on the corner of a 5 x 9-1/2-inch BLACK PRINT rectangle. Draw a diagonal line on the BEIGE PRINT square, and stitch on the line. Trim the seam allowance to 1/4-inch; press. Repeat this process at the opposite corner of the BLACK PRINT rectangle. <u>At this point each roof unit should measure 5 x 9-1/2 inches.</u>

Make 9

2. To assemble each house base, sew a 2 x 3-1/2-inch house fabric rectangle to both sides of a 3-1/2-inch GOLD PRINT square; press. Add a 3-1/2-inch GOLD PRINT square and a 3-1/2-inch house fabric square to the bottom of this unit.

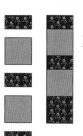

Make 1 from each fabric

Make 9

3. Sew a 3-1/2 x 12-1/2-inch house fabric rectangle to both sides of the Step 2 unit; press.

4. Sew the roof to the top of the house base to complete the house block. <u>At this point each house block should measure 9-1/2 x 17 inches.</u>

Make 9

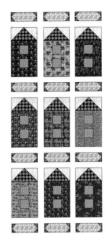

Quilt Center

Cutting

From **TAN PRINT** cut

- 9—3-1/2 x 42-inch strips; from the strips cut 12—3-1/2 x 9-1/2-inch rectangles and 12—3-1/2 x 17-inch rectangles.

From **CHESTNUT PRINT** cut

- 2—3-1/2 x 42-inch strips; from the strips cut 16—3-1/2-inch squares.
- 5—2 x 42-inch strips; from the strips cut 96—2-inch squares.

Quilt Center Assembly

1. With right sides together, position a 2-inch CHESTNUT PRINT square on the corner of a 3-1/2 x 9-1/2-inch TAN PRINT rectangle. Draw a diagonal line on the CHESTNUT PRINT square and stitch on the line. Trim seam allowance to 1/4 inch. Press seam allowance toward the CHESTNUT PRINT fabric. Repeat for each of the four corners of the rectangle.

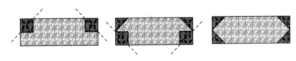

Make 12

2. Sew the lattice units from Step 1 and the house blocks together in three vertical rows alternating the blocks and the lattice strips. Press the seam allowances toward the lattice units. <u>At this point each block row should measure 9-1/2 x 62-inches.</u>

3. With right sides together, position a 2-inch CHESTNUT PRINT square on the corner of a 3-1/2 x 17-inch TAN PRINT rectangle. Draw a line diagonally from corner to corner on the CHESTNUT square. Stitch on this line. Trim seam allowance to 1/4-inch; press. Repeat for the four corners of the rectangle.

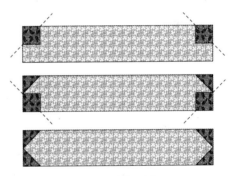

Make 12

4. Sew the lattice units from Step 3 and the 3-1/2-inch CHESTNUT PRINT squares together in four vertical strips, alternating the lattice units and square. Press seam allowances toward the lattice. <u>At this point each lattice strip should measure 3-1/2 x 62-inches.</u>

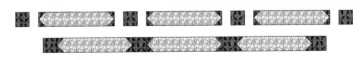

Make 4 lattice strips

5. Sew the block rows and the lattice strips together. Press the seam allowances toward the lattice. <u>At this point the quilt center should measure 39-1/2 x 62-inches.</u>

Borders

Refer to **Binding and Diagonal Piecing** on page 221 for complete instructions with detailed illustrations.

NOTE: The yardage given allows for the middle border strips to be cut on the crosswise grain and for the outer border strips to be cut on the lengthwise grain.

Cutting

From **BEIGE PRINT** cut

- 6 or 7—2 x 42-inch strips; from the strips cut
  6—2 x 17-inch rectangles,
  6—2 x 9-1/2-inch rectangles,
  16—2 x 3-1/2-inch rectangles and
  4—2-inch squares.

From **CHESTNUT PRINT** cut

- 2—2 x 42-inch strips; from the strips cut
  32—2-inch squares.

From **DARK GREEN PRINT** cut

- 6—2 x 42-inch strips for middle border.
- 4—6-1/2-inch squares for corner blocks.

From **TAN LEAF PRINT** cut

- 2—6-1/2 x 70-inch strips for side outer borders (cut on lengthwise grain).
- 2—6-1/2 x 47-inch strips for top and bottom outer borders (cut on lengthwise grain).

Attaching the Borders

1. With right sides together, position a 2-inch CHESTNUT PRINT square on the corner of a 2 x 3-1/2-inch BEIGE PRINT rectangle. Draw a diagonal line on the CHESTNUT PRINT square and stitch on the line. Trim seam allowance to 1/4 inch; press. Repeat this process at the opposite corner of the BEIGE PRINT rectangle.

Make 16

2. For the top and bottom inner border strips, sew four units from Step 1; and 3, 2 x 9-1/2-inch BEIGE PRINT rectangles together; press. Sew these strips to the top and bottom of the quilt; press.

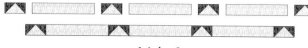

Make 2

3. For the side inner border strips, sew 4 units from Step 1; and 3, 2 x 17-inch BEIGE PRINT rectangles together. Add a 2-inch BEIGE PRINT square to each end. Sew these strips to the sides of the quilt; press. <u>At this point the quilt should measure 42 x 64-1/2-inches.</u>

4. Measure the quilt from left to right through the center to determine the length of the top and bottom middle border strips. Cut 2, 2-inch wide DARK GREEN PRINT strips to this measurement and pin them to the top and bottom of the quilt. Sew the strips to the quilt and press the seam allowances toward the border.

5. Measure the quilt from top to bottom through the center, including the border strips just added, to determine the length of the side middle border strips. Cut 2, 2-inch wide DARK GREEN PRINT strips to this measurement and pin them to the sides of the quilt. Sew the strips to the quilt and press the seam allowances toward the border.

6. Measure the quilt from left to right through the center to determine the length of the top and bottom middle border strips. Cut 2, 6-1/2-inch wide TAN LEAF PRINT strips to this measurement and pin them to the top and bottom of the quilt. Sew the strips to the quilt and press the seam allowances toward the border.

7. Measure the quilt from the top to bottom through the center, including the seam allowances but not the border strips just added, to determine the length of the side outer border strips. Cut 2, 6-1/2-inch wide TAN LEAF PRINT strips to this measurement. Sew a 6-1/2-inch DARK GREEN PRINT corner square to each end. Pin and sew the strips to the quilt and press the seam allowances toward the border.

Putting It All Together

Cut the 3-3/4 yard length of backing fabric in half crosswise to make 2, 1-7/8 yards lengths.

Refer to **Finishing the Quilt** on page 221 for complete instructions.

Binding the Quilt

Refer to **Binding and Diagonal Piecing** on page 221 for complete instructions with detailed illustrations.

NOTE: *The 2-3/4-inch strips will produce a 1/2-inch-wide finished double binding. If you would like a wider or narrower binding, adjust the width of the strips you cut.*

Cutting

From **CHESTNUT PRINT** cut
- 8—2-3/4 x 42-inch strips.

Sew the binding to the quilt using a 3/8-inch seam allowance.

Tall Houses

All Star Throw

Staggered blocks of stars alternating with blocks of color are surprisingly simple to piece and provide the perfect wrap up for a cozy evening at home.

All Star Throw

Quilt measures 68 x 76 inches.
Block measures 8 inches square.

*If using flannel, refer to **Helpful Hints for Sewing with Flannel** on page 219.*

Fabric & Supplies

1-1/4 yards	**RED PRINT** for stars and fence border
1 yard	**GREEN PRINT #1** for stars and fence border
1-1/3 yards	**BEIGE PRINT** for star and fence background
2/3 yard	**GREEN/TAN/RED** PLAID for alternate blocks
2/3 yard	**RED/GREEN PLAID** for alternate blocks
1/4 yard	**GREEN PRINT #2** for corner squares
2-1/3 yards	**GREEN FLORAL** for outer border (cut lengthwise)
2 yards	**RED PLAID** for binding (cut on bias)
4 yards	Backing fabric*
Quilt batting	72 x 80 inches

Optional Pieced Backing*

1/3 yard	**GREEN PRINT #1** for stars
1/4 yard	**BEIGE PRINT** for star background
5/8 yard	**GREEN/TAN/RED PLAID** for pieced strip
3-7/8 yards	**RED PRINT** for pieced back

*NOTE: read **Getting Started**, page 216, before beginning this project.*

Star Blocks

Make 9 RED PRINT Blocks
Make 4 GREEN PRINT #1 Blocks

Cutting

From **RED PRINT** cut
- 1—4-1/2 x 42-inch strip; from the strip cut 9—4-1/2-inch squares.
- 5—2-1/2 x 42-inch strips; from the strips cut 72—2-1/2-inch squares.

From **GREEN PRINT #1** cut
- 1—4-1/2 x 42-inch strip; from the strip cut 4—4-1/2-inch squares.
- 2—2-1/2 x 42-inch strips; from the strips cut 32—2-1/2-inch squares.

From **BEIGE PRINT** cut
- 10—2-1/2 x 42-inch strips; from the strips cut 52—2-1/2 x 4-1/2-inch rectangles and 52—2-1/2-inch squares.

Piecing

1. Position a 2-1/2-inch RED PRINT square on the corner of a 2-1/2 x 4-1/2-inch BEIGE PRINT rectangle. Draw a diagonal line on the RED PRINT square and stitch on the line. Trim the seam allowance to 1/4-inch; press. Repeat this process at the opposite corner of the BEIGE PRINT rectangle.

Make 36 star points

2. Sew Step 1 star points to the top and bottom of a 4-1/2-inch RED PRINT square; press.

Make 9

3. Sew 2-1/2-inch BEIGE PRINT squares to the sides of the remaining star points; press. At this point each RED PRINT star block should measure 8-1/2-inches square.

Make 9

4. To make the GREEN PRINT #1 star blocks, repeat Steps 1, 2, and 3 using the 2-1/2-inch and 4-1/2-inch GREEN PRINT #1 squares, and the remaining 2-1/2-inch BEIGE PRINT squares, and 2-1/2 x 4-1/2-inch BEIGE PRINT rectangles. At this point each GREEN PRINT #1 star block should measure 8-1/2-inches square.

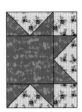

Make 4

Quilt Center

Cutting

From **RED/GREEN PLAID** cut
- 2—8-1/2 x 42-inch strips; from the strips cut 6—8-1/2 x 12-1/2-inch rectangles.

From **GREEN/TAN/RED PLAID** cut
- 2—8-1/2 x 42-inch strips; from the strips cut 2—8-1/2 x 12-1/2-inch rectangles and 4—8-1/2 x 10-1/2-inch rectangles.

Quilt Center Assembly

1. Referring to the quilt illustration for block placement, sew 3 RED PRINT star blocks and 2, 8-1/2 x 12-1/2-inch RED/GREEN PLAID rectangles together in vertical block rows; press. Make 3 block rows. At this point each block row should measure 8-1/2 x 48-1/2 inches.

2. Referring to the quilt illustration for block placement, sew 2 GREEN PRINT #1 star blocks, 1, 8-1/2 x 12-1/2-inch GREEN/TAN/RED PLAID rectangle, and 2, 8-1/2 x 10-1/2-inch GREEN/TAN/RED PLAID rectangles together in vertical block rows, press. Make 2 block rows. At this point each block row should measure 8-1/2 x 48-1/2 inches.

3. Referring to the quilt illustration, pin the block rows together at the block intersections. Sew the rows together; press. At this point the quilt center should measure 40-1/2 x 48-1/2 inches.

Fence Border

Cutting

From **RED PRINT** cut
- 3—4-1/2 x 42-inch strips; from the strips cut 18—4-1/2 x 6-1/2-inch rectangles.
- 2—2-1/2 x 42-inch strips; from the strips cut 8—2-1/2 x 6-1/2-inch rectangles.

From **GREEN PRINT #1** cut
- 4—4-1/2 x 42-inch strips; from the strips cut 22—4-1/2 x 6-1/2-inch rectangles.

From **BEIGE PRINT** cut
- 6—2-1/2 x 42-inch strips; from the strips cut 88—2-1/2-inch squares.

From **GREEN PRINT #2** cut
- 1—6-1/2 x 42-inch strip; from the strip cut 4—6-1/2-inch corner squares.

Attaching the Fence Border

1. Position a 2-1/2-inch BEIGE PRINT square on the corner of a 4-1/2 x 6-1/2-inch RED PRINT rectangle. Draw a diagonal line on the BEIGE PRINT square and stitch on the line. Trim the seam allowance to 1/4-inch; press. Repeat this process at the adjacent corner of the RED PRINT rectangle. At this point each fence unit should measure 4-1/2 x 6-1/2 inches.

Make 18 RED PRINT fence units

2. Position a 2-1/2-inch BEIGE PRINT square on the corner of a 4-1/2 x 6-1/2-inch GREEN PRINT #1 rectangle. Draw a diagonal line on the BEIGE PRINT square and stitch on the line. Trim the seam allowance to 1/4-inch; press. Repeat this process at

the adjacent corner of the GREEN PRINT #1 rectangle. <u>At this point each fence unit should measure 4-1/2 x 6-1/2-inches.</u>

Make 22 GREEN PRINT #1 fence units

3. Position a 2-1/2-inch BEIGE PRINT square on the corner of a 2-1/2 x 6-1/2-inch RED PRINT rectangle. Draw a diagonal line on the BEIGE PRINT square and stitch on the line. Trim the seam allowance to 1/4-inch; press. <u>At this point each fence unit should measure 2-1/2 x 6-1/2 inches.</u>

Make 4

4. Repeat Step 3 but reverse the direction of the drawn sewing line.

Make 4

5. For the top and bottom fence border strips, sew together 4, 4-1/2 x 6-1/2-inch RED PRINT fence units and 5, 4-1/2 x 6-1/2-inch GREEN PRINT #1 fence units. Add a 2-1/2 x 6-1/2-inch RED PRINT fence unit to each end of the strip; press. <u>At this point each fence border should measure 6-1/2 x 40-1/2-inches.</u> Sew the strips to the top and bottom of the quilt center; press.

Make 2

6. For the side fence border strips, sew together 5, 4-1/2 x 6-1/2-inch RED PRINT fence units and 6, 4-1/2 x 6-1/2-inch GREEN PRINT #1 fence units. Add a 2-1/2 x 6-1/2-inch RED PRINT fence unit to each end of the strips. Add a 6-1/2-inch GREEN PRINT #2 corner square to each end of the strips; press. <u>At this point each fence border should measure 6-1/2 x 60-1/2 inches.</u> Sew the strips to the sides of the quilt center; press.

Make 2

Outer Border

NOTE: *The yardage given allows for the border strips to be cut on the lengthwise grain.*

Cutting

From **GREEN FLORAL** cut
- 2—8-1/2 x 80-inch side outer border strips.
- 2—8-1/2 x 54-inch top and bottom outer border strips.

Attaching the Border

1. Measure the quilt from left to right through the center to determine the length of the top and bottom inner border strips. Cut 2, 8-1/2 x 54-inch GREEN FLORAL strips to this measurement and pin them to the top and bottom of the quilt. Sew the strips to the quilt and press the seam allowances toward the border.

2. Measure the quilt from the top to bottom through the center, including the border strips just added, to determine the length of the side outer border strips. Cut 2, 8-1/2 x 80-inch GREEN FLORAL strips to this measurement and pin them to the sides of the quilt. Sew the strips to the quilt and press the seam allowances toward the border.

Putting It All Together

Cut the 4 yard length of backing fabric in half crosswise to make 2, 2 yard lengths.

Refer to **Finishing the Quilt** on page 221 for complete instructions.

*To make the **Optional Pieced Backing** see the instructions below.

Optional Pieced Backing

Cutting

From **GREEN PRINT #1** cut
- 1—4-1/2 x 42-inch strip; from the strip cut 3—4-1/2-inch squares and 8—2-1/2-inch squares.
- 1—2-1/2 x 42-inch strip; from the strip cut 16—2-1/2-inch squares.

From **BEIGE PRINT** cut
- 2—2-1/2 x 42-inch strips; from the strips cut 12—2-1/2 x 4-1/2-inch rectangles and 12—2-1/2-inch squares.

From **GREEN/TAN/RED PLAID** cut
- 2—8-1/2 x 42-inch strips; from the strips cut 2—8-1/2 x 16-1/2-inch rectangles and 2—8-1/2 x 12-1/2-inch rectangles.

From **RED PRINT** cut
- 1—2-2/3-yard length and set aside.
- 2—18-1/2 x 40-1/2-inch strips.

Piecing

1. Position a 2-1/2-inch GREEN PRINT #1 square on the corner of a 2-1/2 x 4-1/2-inch BEIGE PRINT rectangle. Draw a diagonal line on the GREEN PRINT #1 square and stitch on the line. Trim the seam allowance to 1/4-inch; press. Repeat this process at the opposite corner of the BEIGE PRINT rectangle.

Make 12 star points

2. Sew Step 1 star points to the top and bottom of a 4-1/2-inch GREEN PRINT #1 square; press. Sew 2-1/2-inch BEIGE PRINT squares to the sides of the remaining star points; press. Sew the star points to the sides of the unit; press. <u>At this point each GREEN PRINT #1 star block should measure 8-1/2 inches square.</u>

3. Referring to the backing illustration, sew the star blocks and the 8-1/2 x 12-1/2-inch GREEN/TAN/RED PLAID rectangles together.

Sew the 8-1/2 x 16-1/2-inch GREEN/TAN/RED PLAID rectangles to both ends of the strip; press. <u>At this point the strip should measure 8-1/2 x 80-1/2 inches.</u>

Make 3

4. Referring to the backing illustration, sew the 18-1/2 x 40-1/2-inch RED PRINT strips together; press. Sew this unit to the Step 3 pieced strip, press.

5. Cut the 2-2/3 yard length of backing fabric in half crosswise to form 2, 1-1/3 yard lengths. Remove the selvages from the backing fabric, sew the long edges together; press. Trim the unit to 46-1/2 x 80-1/2-inches. Sew the unit to the Step 4 unit; press.

Binding the Quilt

Refer to **Binding and Diagonal Piecing** on page 221 for complete instructions with detailed illustrations

NOTE: The 6-1/2-inch strips will produce a 1-inch wide finished double binding. If you would like a wider or narrower binding, adjust the width of the strips you cut.

Cutting

From **RED PLAID** cut
- 6-1/2-inch wide bias strips to make a strip approximately 310-inches long.

Sew the binding to the quilt using a scant 1-inch seam allowance.

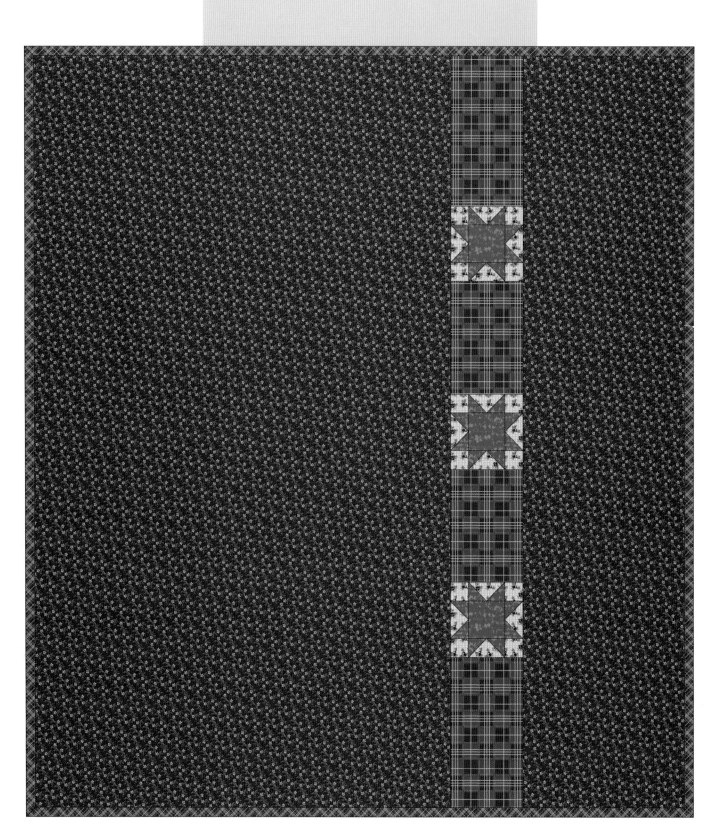

All Star Throw

Optional Pieced Backing

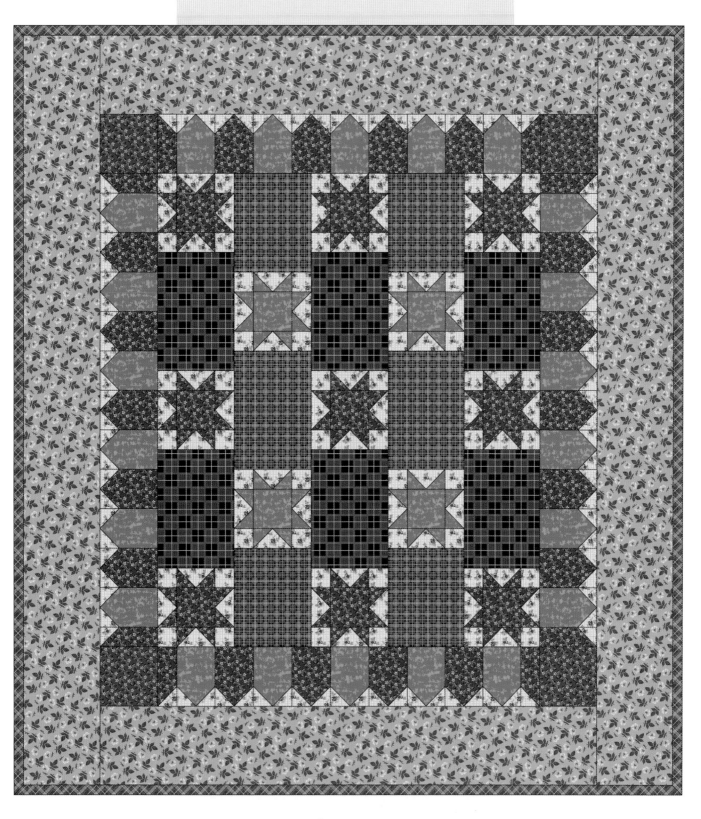

All Star Throw

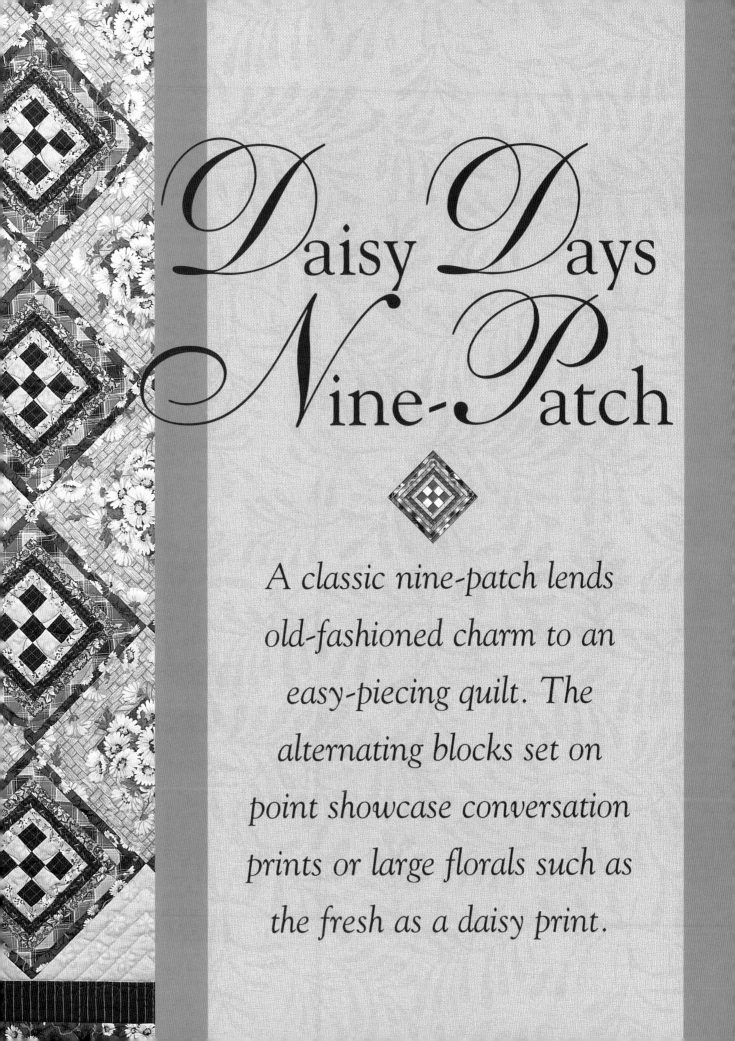

Daisy Days Nine-Patch

A classic nine-patch lends
old-fashioned charm to an
easy-piecing quilt. The
alternating blocks set on
point showcase conversation
prints or large florals such as
the fresh as a daisy print.

Daisy Days Nine-Patch

Quilt measures 65 x 76 inches.
Block measures 8 inches square.

Fabric & Supplies

1/3 yard	**BLUE PLAID** for nine-patch units
1 yard	**BEIGE PRINT** for nine-patch units and side and corner triangles
1/3 yard	**YELLOW PRINT** for blocks
3/8 yard	**RED PRINT** for blocks
1/2 yard	**LIGHT BLUE PRINT** for blocks
1/2 yard	**RED/BLUE DIAGONAL PRINT** for blocks
2-1/3 yards	**BLUE FLORAL** for blocks and outer border
1-7/8 yards	**BEIGE DAISY BASKET** for alternate blocks. This extra yardage allows for the cluster of flowers to be centered in each alternate block.
1/2 yard	**RED STRIPE** for inner border
3/4 yard	**RED STRIPE** for binding
4 yards	Backing fabric
Quilt batting	69 x 80 inches

NOTE: read **Getting Started**,
page 216, before beginning this project.

Nine-Patch Blocks

Make 20 Blocks

Cutting

From **BLUE PLAID** cut
• 5—1-1/2 x 42-inch strips.

From **BEIGE PRINT** cut
• 4—1-1/2 x 42-inch strips.

From **YELLOW PRINT** cut
• 10—1 x 42-inch strips.

From **RED PRINT** cut
• 11—1 x 42-inch strips.

From **LIGHT BLUE PRINT** cut
• 13—1 x 42-inch strips.

From **RED/BLUE DIAGONAL PRINT** cut
• 15—1 x 42-inch strips.

From **BLUE FLORAL** cut
• 17—1 x 42-inch strips.

Piecing

1. Aligning long edges, sew 1-1/2 x 42-inch BLUE PLAID strips to both sides of a 1-1/2 x 42-inch BEIGE PRINT strip; press. Make a total of 2 strip sets. Cut the strip sets into segments.

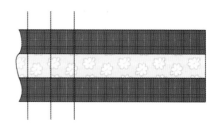

Crosscut 40—1-1/2-inch wide segments

2. Aligning long edges, sew 1-1/2 x 42-inch BEIGE PRINT strips to both sides of a 1-1/2 x 42-inch BLUE PLAID strip; press. Cut the strip set into segments.

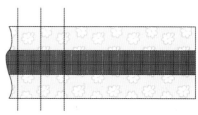

Crosscut 20—1-1/2-inch wide segments

3. Sew a Step 1 segment at the top and bottom of a Step 2 segment; press. At this point each nine-patch unit should measure 3-1/2 inches square.

Make 20 Nine-Patch units

4. Aligning long edges, sew a 1-inch wide YELLOW PRINT strip to the top and bottom of the nine-patch unit. Press the seam allowance toward the strips. Trim the strips even with the edges of the nine-patch unit.

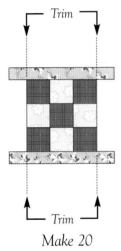

Make 20

5. Aligning long edges, sew a 1-inch wide YELLOW PRINT strip to the sides of the nine-patch unit. Press the seam allowances toward the strips. Trim the strips even with the edges of the nine-patch unit.

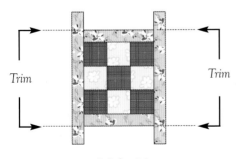

Make 20

6. Referring to the block illustration, continue this process by adding 1-inch wide RED PRINT strips, LIGHT BLUE PRINT strips, RED/BLUE

DIAGONAL PRINT strips, and BLUE FLORAL strips to complete the block. Press each seam allowance toward the strip just added, and trim each strip before adding the next. Each block should measure 8-1/2 inches square when complete.

Make 20

Quilt Center

NOTE: The side and corner triangles are larger than necessary and will be trimmed before the borders are added.

Cutting

From **BEIGE DAISY BASKET** cut
- 12—8-1/2-inch squares, taking care to center a cluster of flowers in the center of each alternate block, *or* cut
- 3—8-1/2 x 42-inch strips; from the strips cut 12—8-1/2-inch alternate block squares.

From **BEIGE PRINT** cut
- 2—13 x 42-inch strips. From these strips cut 4—13-inch squares. Cut the squares diagonally into quarters for a total of 16 triangles. You will be using only 14 for side triangles. 2—8-inch squares. Cut the squares in half diagonally for a total of 4 corner triangles.

Quilt Center Assembly

1. Referring to the quilt assembly illustration for block placement, sew together the pieced blocks, 8-1/2-inch alternate blocks, and side triangles in 8 diagonal rows. Press the seam allowances toward the alternate blocks and side triangles.

2. Pin the rows together at the block intersections and sew together. Press the seam allowance in one direction.

3. Sew the corner triangles to the quilt center; press.

4. Trim away the excess fabric from the side and corner triangles taking care to allow a 1/4-inch seam allowance beyond the corners of each block.

Refer to **Trimming Side and Corner Triangles** on page 218 for complete instructions.

Borders

Refer to **Binding and Diagonal Piecing** on page 221 for complete instructions with detailed illustrations.

NOTE: The yardage given allows for the border strips to be cut on the crosswise grain.

Cutting

From **RED STRIPE** cut
- 6—2-1/2 x 42-inch inner border strips.

From **BLUE FLORAL** cut
- 7—8-1/2 x 42-inch outer border strips.

Attaching the Borders

1. Measure the quilt from left to right through the center to determine the length of the top and bottom inner border strips. Cut 2, 2-1/2-inch wide RED STRIPE strips to this measurement and pin them to the top and bottom of the quilt.

Sew the strips to the quilt and press the seam allowances toward the border.

2. Measure the quilt from the top to bottom through the center, including the border strips just added, to determine the length of the side inner border strips. Cut 2, 2-1/2-inch wide RED STRIPE strips to this measurement and pin them to the sides of the quilt. Sew the strips to the quilt and press the seam allowances toward the border.

3. Measure the quilt from left to right through the center to determine the length of the top and bottom outer border strips. Cut 2, 8-1/2-inch wide BLUE FLORAL strips to this measurement and pin them to the top and bottom of the quilt. Sew the strips to the quilt and press the seam allowances toward the border.

4. Measure the quilt from top to bottom through the center to determine the length of the side outer border strips. Cut 2, 8-1/2-inch wide BLUE FLORAL strips to this measurement and pin them to the sides of the quilt. Sew the strips to the quilt and press the seam allowances toward the border.

Putting It All Together

Cut the 4-yard length of backing fabric in half crosswise to make 2, 2-yard lengths.

Refer to **Finishing the Quilt** on page 221 for complete instructions.

Binding the Quilt

Refer to **Binding and Diagonal Piecing** on page 221 for complete instructions with detailed illustrations.

NOTE: The 2-3/4-inch strips will produce a 1/2-inch wide finished double binding. If you would like a wider or narrower binding, adjust the width of the strips you cut.

Cutting

From RED STRIPE cut
- 8—2-3/4 x 42-inch strips.

Sew the binding to the quilt using a 3/8-inch seam allowance.

Daisy Days Nine-Patch

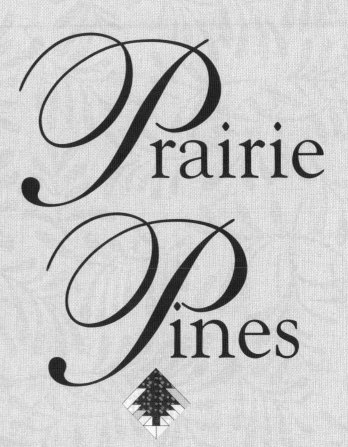

Prairie Pines

What can only be described as
a classic Thimbleberries®
quilt—a multi-print border
surrounding a traditional
setting of pieced pine trees gives
the soft suggestion of light
filtering through the forest.

Prairie Pines

Quilt measures 65 x 80 inches.
Block measures 9-1/2 inches square.

Fabric & Supplies

1/4 yard	**ASSORTED BEIGE PRINTS** (10 prints) for background
1-1/2 yards	**GREEN PRINT** for trees
1/4 yard	**BROWN PRINT** for tree trunks
1 yard	**BEIGE FLORAL** for side and corner triangles
1/2 yard	**RED PRINT** for inner border
5/8 yard	**GREEN HOLLY PRINT** for middle border
2-1/4 yards	**POSTCARD PRINT** for outer border
3/4 yard	**RED PRINT** for binding
4 yards	Backing fabric
Quilt batting	69 x 84 inches

NOTE: *read* **Getting Started**, *page 216, before beginning this project.*

Pine Tree Blocks

Make 18 Blocks

Cutting

From **ASSORTED BEIGE PRINTS** cut
- 36 of Pattern E.
- 36 of Pattern F.
- 54 of Pattern G.
- 54 of Pattern G reversed.
- 18 of Pattern H.
- 18 of Pattern H reversed.

From **GREEN PRINT** cut
- 72 of Pattern A.
- 36 of Pattern B.
- 36 of Pattern C.

From **BROWN PRINT** cut
- 18 of Pattern D.
- 18 of Pattern D reversed.

Piecing

1. For one pine tree block, you will need
    4 GREEN PRINT A pieces,
    2 GREEN PRINT B pieces,
    2 GREEN PRINT C pieces,
    1 BROWN PRINT D piece,
    1 BROWN PRINT D reversed piece,
    2 BEIGE PRINT E triangles,
    2 BEIGE PRINT F triangles,
    3 BEIGE PRINT G pieces,
    3 BEIGE PRINT G reversed pieces,
    1 BEIGE PRINT H piece, and
    1 BEIGE PRINT H reversed piece.

2. Referring to the illustration, sew together a BEIGE PRINT H piece and a GREEN PRINT A piece. Press the seam allowance toward the GREEN PRINT. In the same manner sew together
    GREEN PRINT B piece to a
    BEIGE PRINT G piece,
    GREEN PRINT A piece to a
    BEIGE PRINT G piece,
    GREEN PRINT C piece to a
    BEIGE PRINT G piece,
    BROWN PRINT D piece to a
    BEIGE PRINT E triangle,
    GREEN PRINT A piece to a
    BEIGE PRINT H reversed piece,

GREEN PRINT B piece to a
BEIGE PRINT G reversed piece,
GREEN PRINT A piece to a
BEIGE PRINT G reversed piece,
GREEN PRINT C piece to a
BEIGE PRINT G reversed piece, and
BROWN PRINT D reversed piece to a
BEIGE PRINT E triangle.

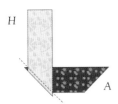

3. Referring to the illustration for placement, sew together 5 pieced strips for each half of the tree. Press the seam allowances toward the top of the tree on the left-hand side and toward the bottom of the tree on the right-hand side. Sew a BEIGE PRINT F triangle to the bottom of each tree half; press.

4. Pin the tree halves together at the seam lines and sew. Press the center seam allowance open. Square off all blocks so they are the same measurement. The blocks should be approximately 10-inches square.

Make 18

Quilt Center

NOTE: *The side and corner triangles are larger than necessary and will be trimmed before the borders are added.*

Cutting

From **BEIGE FLORAL** cut

- 2—15-1/2 x 42-inch strips; from the strips cut 3—15-1/2-inch squares. Cut each square into quarters diagonally to make 12 triangles. (NOTE: You will be using only 10 for side triangles.)
- 2—9-inch squares. Cut each square in half diagonally for a total of 4 corner triangles.

Quilt Center Assembly

1. Referring to the quilt illustration for block placement, sew the pieced tree blocks and BEIGE FLORAL side triangles together in diagonal rows. Press the seam allowances in alternating directions by rows so the seams will fit snugly together with less bulk.

2. Pin the rows at the block intersections and sew the rows together. Press the seam allowances in one direction.

3. Sew the BEIGE FLORAL corner triangles to the quilt center; press.

4. Trim away excess fabric from side and corner triangles, taking care to allow a 1/4-inch seam allowance beyond the corners of each block.

Refer to **Trimming Side and Corner Triangles** on page 218 for complete instructions.

Borders

Refer to **Binding and Diagonal Piecing** on page 221 for complete instructions with detailed illustrations.

NOTE: *The yardage given allows for the border strips to be cut on the crosswise grain. Diagonally piece the strips as needed.*

Cutting

From **RED PRINT** cut

- 5—2-1/2 x 42-inch inner border strips.

From **GREEN HOLLY PRINT** cut

- 7—2-1/2 x 42-inch middle border strips.

From **POSTCARD PRINT** cut

- 8—8-1/2 x 42-inch outer border strips.

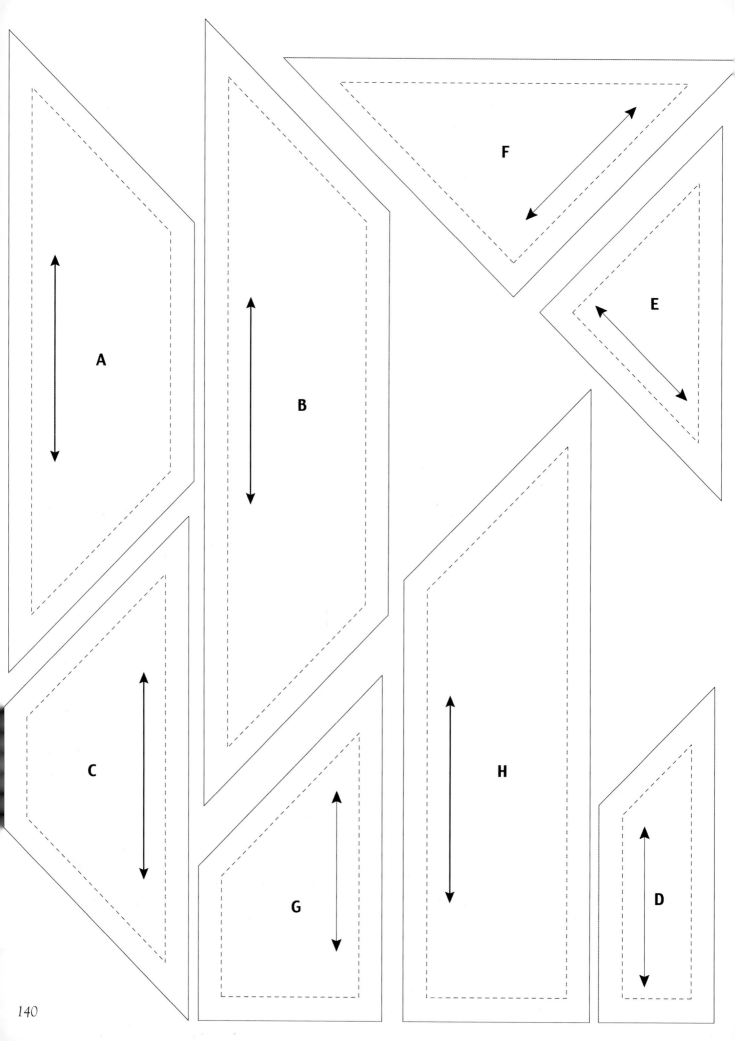

A

B

C

D

E

F

G

H

140

Attaching the Borders

1. Measure the quilt from left to right through the center to determine the length of the top and bottom inner border strips. Cut 2, 2-1/2-inch wide RED PRINT strips to this measurement and pin them to the top and bottom of the quilt. Sew the strips to the quilt and press the seam allowances toward the border.

2. Measure the quilt from the top to bottom through the center, including the border strips just added, to determine the length of the side inner border strips. Cut 2, 2-1/2-inch wide RED PRINT strips to this measurement. Pin and sew the strips to the quilt and press the seam allowances toward the border.

3. Measure the quilt from left to right through the center to determine the length of the top and bottom middle border strips. Cut 2, 2-1/2-inch wide GREEN HOLLY strips to this measurement and pin them to the top and bottom of the quilt. Sew the strips to the quilt and press the seam allowances toward the border.

4. Measure the quilt from the top to bottom through the center, including the border strips just added, to determine the length of the side middle border strips. Cut 2, 2-1/2-inch wide GREEN HOLLY strips to this measurement. Pin and sew the strips to the quilt and press the seam allowances toward the border.

5. Measure the quilt from left to right through the center to determine the length of the top and bottom outer border strips. Cut 2, 8-1/2-inch wide POST CARD PRINT strips to this measurement and pin them to the top and bottom of the quilt. Sew the strips to the quilt and press the seam allowances toward the border.

6. Measure the quilt from the top to bottom through the center, including the border strips just added, to determine the length of the side outer border strips. Cut 2, 8-1/2-inch wide POST CARD PRINT strips to this measurement. Pin and sew the strips to the quilt and press the seam allowances toward the border.

Putting It All Together

Cut the 4-yard length of backing fabric in half crosswise to make 2, 2-yard lengths.

Refer to **Finishing the Quilt** on page 221 for complete instructions.

Binding the Quilt

Refer to **Binding and Diagonal Piecing** on page 221 for complete instructions with detailed illustrations.

NOTE: *The 2-3/4-inch strips will produce a 1/2-inch wide finished double binding. If you would like a wider or narrower binding, adjust the width of the strips you cut.*

Cutting

From RED PRINT cut
- 8—2-3/4 x 42-inch strips.

Sew the binding to the quilt using a 3/8-inch seam allowance.

Flower Patch Throw

Alternating blocks of plaid
add another level of design
to the pieced block with dark
corners which create an
additional connecting design
for a cottage garden quilt
with multi-faceted appeal.

Quilt measures 66 x 77 inches.
Block measures 8 inches square.

Fabric & Supplies

7/8 yard	**BEIGE PRINT** for blocks
3/4 yard	**GREEN PRINT** for blocks
2/3 yard	**GREEN DAISY BASKET** for center squares. Extra yardage allows for the daisy cluster to be centered in each square.
1/2 yard	**BLUE PLAID** for blocks
1-5/8 yards	**BLUE/GREEN PLAID** for side and corner triangles and alternate blocks
1/2 yard	**COCOA PRINT** for inner border
2-1/3 yards	**GREEN FLORAL** for outer border (cut lengthwise)
3/4 yard	**BLUE PLAID** for binding (cut on bias)
4 yards	Backing fabric
Quilt batting	70 x 81 inches

NOTE: read **Getting Started**,
page 216, before beginning this project.

Pieced Blocks

Make 20 Blocks

Cutting

From **BEIGE PRINT** cut
- 10—2-1/2 x 42-inch strips; from the strips cut 160—2-1/2-inch squares.

From **GREEN PRINT** cut
- 9—2-1/2 x 42-inch strips; from the strips cut 80—2-1/2 x 4-1/2-inch rectangles.

From **GREEN DAISY BASKET** cut
- 20—4-1/2-inch squares, taking care to center a cluster of flowers in the center of each square, or 3—4-1/2 x 42-inch strips; from the strips cut 20—4-1/2-inch squares.

From **BLUE PLAID** cut
- 5—2-1/2 x 42-inch strips; from the strips cut 80—2-1/2-inch squares.

Piecing

1. Position a 2-1/2-inch BEIGE PRINT square on the corner of a 2-1/2 x 4-1/2-inch GREEN PRINT rectangle. Draw a diagonal line on the BEIGE PRINT square and stitch on the line. Trim the seam allowance to 1/4-inch; press. Repeat this process at the opposite corner of the GREEN PRINT rectangle.

Make 80

2. Sew a Step 1 segment to the top and bottom of a 4-1/2-inch GREEN DAISY BASKET square; press. Add 2-1/2-inch BLUE PLAID squares to the remaining Step 1 units; press. Sew these units to the sides of the square; press. At this point each block should measure 8-1/2 inches square.

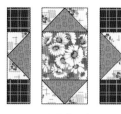

Make 20

Quilt Center

NOTE: The side and corner triangles are larger than necessary and will be trimmed before the borders are added.

Cutting

From **BLUE/GREEN PLAID** cut
- 2—13 x 42-inch strips; from the strips cut 4—13-inch squares. Cut the squares diagonally into quarters for a total of 16 triangles. You will be using only 14 for side triangles.
- 2—8-inch squares. Cut the squares in half diagonally for a total of 4 corner triangles.
- 3—8-1/2 x 42-inch strips; from the strips cut 12—8-1/2-inch alternate block squares.

Quilt Center Assembly

1. Referring to the quilt assembly illustration for block placement, sew together the pieced blocks, 8-1/2-inch alternate blocks, and side triangles in 8 diagonal rows. Press the seam allowances toward the alternate blocks and side triangles.

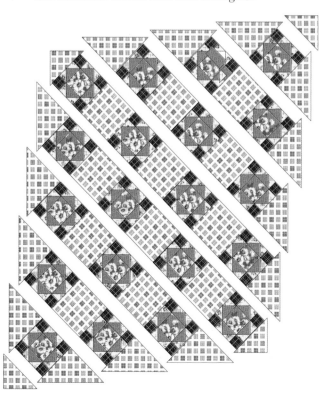

2. Pin the rows together at the block intersections and sew together. Press the seam allowances in one direction.

3. Sew the corner triangles to the quilt center; press.

4. Trim away the excess fabric from the side and corner triangles taking care to allow a 1/4-inch seam allowance beyond the corners of each block.

Refer to **Trimming Side and Corner Triangles** on page 218 for complete instructions.

Borders

Refer to **Binding and Diagonal Piecing** on page 221 for complete instructions with detailed illustrations.

NOTE: The yardage given allows for the inner border strips to be cut on the crosswise grain and for the outer border strips to be cut on the lengthwise grain.

Cutting

From **COCOA PRINT** cut
- 6—2-1/2 x 42-inch inner border strips.

From **GREEN FLORAL** cut
- 2—8-1/2 x 81-inch side outer border strips (cut on lengthwise grain).
- 2—8-1/2 x 54-inch top/bottom outer border strips (cut on lengthwise grain).

Attaching the Borders

1. Measure the quilt from left to right through the center to determine the length of the top and bottom inner border strips. Cut 2, 2-1/2-inch wide COCOA PRINT strips to this measurement and pin them to the top and bottom of the quilt. Sew the strips to the quilt and press the seam allowances toward the border.

2. Measure the quilt from the top to bottom through the center, including the border strips just added, to determine the length of the side inner border strips. Cut 2, 2-1/2-inch wide COCOA PRINT strips to this measurement. Pin and sew the strips to the quilt and press the seam allowances toward the border.

3. Measure the quilt from left to right through the center to determine the length of the top and bottom outer border strips. Cut 2, 8-1/2 x 54-inch GREEN FLORAL strips to this measurement. Pin and sew the strips to the quilt and press the seam allowances toward the border.

4. Measure the quilt from the top to bottom through the center, including the border strips just added, to determine the length of the side outer border strips. Cut 2, 8-1/2 x 81-inch GREEN FLORAL strips to this measurement. Pin and sew the strips to the quilt and press the seam allowances toward the border.

Putting It All Together

Cut the 4-yard length of backing fabric in half crosswise to make 2, 2-yard lengths.

Refer to **Finishing the Quilt** on page 221 for complete instructions.

Binding the Quilt

Refer to **Binding and Diagonal Piecing** on page 221 for complete instructions with detailed illustrations.

NOTE: *The 2-3/4-inch strips will produce a 1/2-inch wide finished double binding. If you would like a wider or narrower binding, adjust the width of the strips you cut.*

Cutting

From **BLUE PLAID** cut
- 2-3/4-inch wide bias strips to make a strip approximately 300-inches long.

Sew the binding to the quilt using a 3/8-inch seam allowance.

Flower Patch Throw

Sleeping

BEAUTIES

Transform any room into a restful retreat and take a sabbatical from stress—on a daily basis!

Whether it's breakfast in bed, an afternoon nap, or a blissful evening with a good book, snuggling up in an inviting quilt makes it even more memorable. To fill your rooms with soft comfort, choose from any of the eye-catching quilts featured on the following pages.

Berries & Blossoms

Barn Raising—the classic log cabin block, provides ample opportunity to mix many colors and prints.

The cream background of the vine print used on the outer logs of each block forms another design element within the traditional cabin block setting.

Berries & Blossoms

Quilt measures 80 x 96 inches.
Block measures 8 inches square.

Fabric & Supplies

3/4 yard	**GOLD PRINT** for center squares
1 yard	**CREAM PRINT** for Log Cabin strips
1-1/2 yards	**BEIGE PRINT** for Log Cabin strips
2 yards	**BEIGE BERRY PRINT** for Log Cabin strips
2/3 yard	**CHESTNUT FRUIT PRINT** for Log Cabin strips
3/4 yard	**BROWN FLORAL** for Log Cabin strips
7/8 yard	**GREEN PRINT** for Log Cabin strips
1 yard	**GREEN FRUIT PRINT** for Log Cabin strips
1-1/8 yards	**BRICK FRUIT PRINT** for Log Cabin strips
1-3/8 yards	**BRICK FLORAL** for Log Cabin strips
7/8 yard	**GREEN PRINT** for binding
7 yards	Backing fabric
Quilt batting	84 x 100 inches

NOTE: read **Getting Started**,
page 216, before beginning this project.

Log Cabin Blocks

Make 120 Blocks

Cutting

From **GOLD PRINT** cut
- 8—2-1/2 x 42-inch strips.

From **CREAM PRINT** cut
- 21—1-1/2 x 42-inch strips.

From **BEIGE PRINT** cut
- 33—1-1/2 x 42-inch strips.

From **BEIGE BERRY PRINT** cut
- 45—1-1/2 x 42-inch strips.

From **CHESTNUT FRUIT PRINT** cut
- 12—1-1/2 x 42-inch strips.

From **BROWN FLORAL** cut
- 15—1-1/2 x 42-inch strips.

From **GREEN PRINT** cut
- 18—1-1/2 x 42-inch strips.

From **GREEN FRUIT PRINT** cut
- 21—1-1/2 x 42-inch strips.

From **BRICK FRUIT PRINT** cut
- 24—1-1/2 x 42-inch strips.

From **BRICK FLORAL** cut
- 27—1-1/2 x 42-inch strips.

Piecing

1. Aligning long edges, sew 8, 2-1/2-inch wide GOLD PRINT strips and 8, 1-1/2-inch wide CREAM PRINT strips together in pairs; press. Make a total of 8 strip sets. Cut the strip sets into segments.

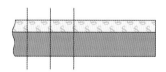

Crosscut 120, 2-1/2-inch wide segments

2. Stitch a 1-1/2-inch wide CREAM PRINT strip to the two-piece unit from Step 1. Press the seam allowance toward the strip. Trim the strip even with the edges of the two-piece unit.

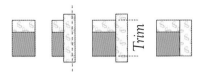

3. Turn the unit a quarter turn to the left. Stitch a 1-1/2-inch wide CHESTNUT FRUIT PRINT strip to the unit. Press and trim the strip even with edges of the unit.

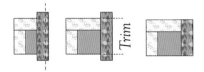

4. Turn the unit a quarter turn to the left. Stitch a 1-1/2-inch wide BROWN FLORAL strip to the unit. Press and trim the strip even with the edges of the unit.

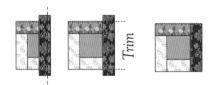

5. Turn the unit a quarter turn to the left. Stitch a 1-1/2-inch wide BEIGE PRINT strip to the unit. Press and trim the strip even with the edges of the unit. Turn the unit again to the left and stitch another 1-1/2-inch wide BEIGE PRINT strip to the unit. Press and trim the strip even with the edges of the unit.

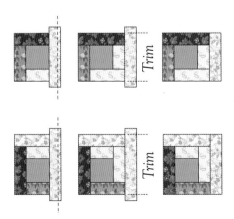

6. Turn the unit again to the left and stitch a 1-1/2-inch wide GREEN PRINT strip to the unit. Press and trim the strip even with the edges of the unit. Turn the unit again to the left and stitch a 1-1/2-inch wide GREEN FRUIT PRINT strip to the unit. Press and trim the strip even with the edges of the unit.

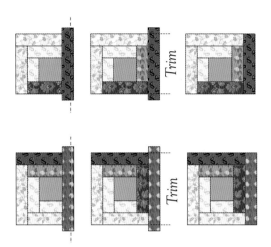

7. Referring to the block diagram, continue this process by adding 1-1/2-inch wide BEIGE BERRY PRINT strips to both sides of the unit. Press each seam allowance toward the strip just added, and trim each strip before adding the next. In the same manner, add the 1-1/2-inch wide BRICK FRUIT strip and the 1-1/2-inch wide BRICK FLORAL strip. Press each seam allowance toward the strip just added, and trim each strip before adding the next. Each Log Cabin block should measure 8-1/2-inches square when completed. Adjust the seam allowances if needed.

NOTE: Follow Steps 1–7 to piece each of the 120 Log Cabin blocks.

Quilt Center

1. Referring to the quilt diagram for block placement, sew the Log Cabin blocks together in 12 rows of 10 blocks each. Press the seam allowances in alternating directions by rows so the seams will fit snugly together with less bulk.

2. Pin the rows at the block intersections and sew the rows together. Press the seam allowances in one direction.

Putting It All Together

Cut the 7-yard length of backing fabric in thirds crosswise to make 3, 2-1/3 yard lengths.

Refer to **Finishing the Quilt** on page 221 for complete instructions.

Binding the Quilt

Refer to **Binding and Diagonal Piecing** on page 221 for complete instructions with detailed illustrations.

NOTE: The 2-3/4-inch strips will produce a 1/2-inch wide finished double binding. If you would like a wider or narrower binding, adjust the width of the strips.

Cutting

From **GREEN PRINT** cut
- 10—2-3/4 x 42-inch strips.

Sew the binding to the quilt using a 3/8-inch seam allowance.

Berries & Blossoms

Christmas Confetti

Big, bright and bold, this easy-to-piece quilt is sure to be the star of your holiday decorating! Long after the tree has been taken down, you can count on Christmas Confetti to chase away the winter doldrums.

Christmas Confetti

Quilt measures 68 x 79 inches.
Block measures 8 inches square.

Fabric & Supplies

2/3 yard	**3 COORDINATING DARK PRINT** fabrics for star blocks (**RED, BLUE,** and **GREEN**)
1-3/4 yards	**BEIGE PRINT** for star background
5/8 yard	**3 COORDINATING DARK PLAID** fabrics for alternate blocks (**RED, BLUE,** and **GOLD**)
7/8 yard	**RED PRINT** for side and corner triangles
1-2/3 yards	**GOLD PRINT** for border
2/3 yard	**BLACK PRINT** for binding
4-2/3 yards	Backing fabric
Quilt batting	72 x 83 inches

NOTE: read **Getting Started**, page 216, before beginning this project.

Star Blocks

Make 30 Blocks (10 from each DARK PRINT)

Cutting

From each **DARK PRINT** cut
- 2—4-1/2 x 42-inch strips; from the strips cut 10—4-1/2-inch squares.
- 5—2-1/2 x 42-inch strips; from the strips cut 80—2-1/2-inch squares.

From **BEIGE PRINT** cut
- 21—2-1/2 x 42-inch strips; from the strips cut 120—2-1/2 x 4-1/2-inch rectangles, and 120—2-1/2-inch squares.

Piecing

1. Position a 2-1/2-inch DARK PRINT square on the corner of a 2-1/2 x 4-1/2-inch BEIGE PRINT rectangle. Draw a diagonal line on the DARK PRINT square, and stitch on this line. Trim the seam allowance to 1/4 inch; press. Repeat this process at the opposite corner of the BEIGE PRINT rectangle.

Make 40 from each DARK PRINT

2. Sew coordinating Step 1 units to the top and bottom of the 4-1/2-inch coordinating squares; press. Sew 2-1/2-inch BEIGE PRINT squares to both sides of the remaining Step 1 units; press. Sew these units to the sides of the coordinating blocks; press. <u>At this point each block should measure 8-1/2 inches square.</u>

Make 10 from each DARK PRINT

Quilt Center

NOTE: *The side and corner triangles are larger than necessary and will be trimmed before the border is added.*

Cutting

From **RED and BLUE PLAIDS** cut
- 2—8-1/2 x 42-inch strips each; from the strips cut 7—8-1/2-inch squares.

From **GOLD PLAID** cut
- 2—8-1/2 x 42-inch strips; from the strips cut 6—8-1/2-inch squares.

From **RED PRINT** cut
- 2—13 x 42-inch strips; from the strips 5—13-inch squares. Cut the squares diagonally into quarters for 20 triangles. You will be using only 18 side triangles.
- 2—8-inch squares. Cut the squares in half diagonally for 4 corner triangles.

Quilt Center Assembly

1. Referring to the quilt diagram, sew the star blocks, the alternate blocks, and the side triangles together in diagonal rows. Press the seam allowances in alternating directions by rows so the seams will fit snugly together with less bulk.

2. Pin the rows at the block intersections, and sew the rows together. Press the seam allowances in one direction.

3. Sew the corner triangles to the quilt; press.

4. Trim away the excess fabric from the side and corner triangles, taking care to allow a 1/4-inch seam allowance beyond the corners of each block.

Refer to **Trimming the Side and Corner Triangles** on page 218 for complete instructions.

Border

Refer to **Binding and Diagonal Piecing** on page 221 for complete instructions with detailed illustrations.

NOTE: *The yardage given allows for the border strips to be cut on the crosswise grain.*

Cutting

From **GOLD PRINT** cut
- 8—6-1/2 x 42-inch border strips.

Attaching the Border

1. Measure the quilt from left to right through the center to determine the length of the top and bottom border strips. Cut 2, 6-1/2-inch wide GOLD PRINT strips to this measurement and pin them to the top and bottom of the quilt. Sew the strips to the quilt and press the seam allowances toward the border.

2. Measure the quilt from the top to bottom through the center, including the border strips just added, to determine the length of the side border strips. Cut 2, 6-1/2-inch wide GOLD PRINT strips to this measurement and pin them to the sides of the quilt. Sew the strips to the quilt and press the seam allowances toward the border.

Putting It All Together

Cut the 4-2/3 yard length of backing fabric in half crosswise to make 2, 2-1/3 yard lengths.

Refer to **Finishing the Quilt** on page 221 for complete instructions.

Binding the Quilt

Refer to **Binding and Diagonal Piecing** on page 221 for complete instructions with detailed illustrations.

NOTE: *The 2-3/4-inch strips will produce a 1/2-inch wide finished double binding. If you would like a wider or narrower binding, adjust the width of the strips.*

Cutting

From **BLACK PRINT** cut
- 8—2-3/4 x 42-inch strips.

Sew the binding to the quilt using a 3/8-inch seam allowance.

Christmas Confetti

159

Courtyard Garden

Create your own bed
of flowers with classic
quilt blocks framed by a
picket fence forming a
cottage garden courtyard
effect around the floral
fantasy of center blocks.

Courtyard Garden

Quilt measures 84 x 96 inches.
Block measures 4 inches square.

Fabric & Supplies

2-1/2 yards **BEIGE PRINT** for quilt center and fence border

4 yards **LARGE FLORAL** for quilt center and outer borders

2 1/8 yards **GREEN PRINT** for quilt center squares, fence background, and outer narrow border

5/8 yard **RED CHECK** for quilt center inner border and corner squares

1 yard **GREEN PLAID** for binding (cut on bias)

7-1/2 yards Backing fabric

Quilt batting 88 x 100 inches

*NOTE: read **Getting Started**, page 216, before beginning this project.*

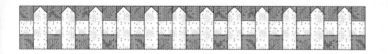

Quilt Center

Cutting

From **BEIGE PRINT** cut
- 8—2-1/2 x 42-inch strips.
- 6—4-1/2 x 42-inch strips.

From **LARGE FLORAL** cut
- 7—4-1/2 x 42-inch strips.

From **GREEN PRINT** cut
- 6—2-1/2 x 42-inch strips.

Piecing

1. Sew a 2-1/2 x 42-inch BEIGE PRINT strip to both sides of a 4-1/2 x 42-inch LARGE FLORAL strip. Press the seam allowances toward the BEIGE PRINT strips. Make 3 strip sets. Cut the strip sets into segments.

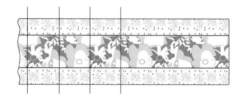

Crosscut 27, 4-1/2-inch wide segments

2. Sew a 4-1/2 x 42-inch LARGE FLORAL strip to both sides of a 2-1/2 x 42-inch BEIGE PRINT strip. Press the seam allowances toward the BEIGE PRINT strip. Make 2 strip sets. Cut the strip sets into segments.

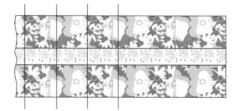

Crosscut 18, 4-1/2-inch wide segments

3. Sew a 2-1/2 x 42-inch GREEN PRINT strip to both sides of a 4-1/2 x 42-inch BEIGE PRINT strip. Make 2 strip sets. Cut the strip sets into segments.

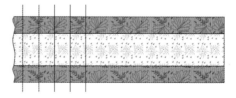

Crosscut 30, 2-1/2-inch wide segments

4. Sew a 4-1/2 x 42-inch BEIGE PRINT strip to both sides of a 2-1/2 x 42-inch GREEN PRINT strip. Press the seam allowances toward the BEIGE PRINT strip. Make 2 strip sets. Cut the strip sets into segments.

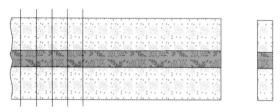

Crosscut 20, 2-1/2-inch wide segments

5. To make the block rows, sew together 3, Step 1 segments and 2, Step 2 segments. Press the seam allowances toward the BEIGE PRINT. Make 9 block rows. Refer to to the quilt illustration on page 165.

6. To make the lattice strips, sew together 3, Step 3 segments and 2, Step 4 segments. Press the seam allowances toward the BEIGE PRINT. Make 10 lattice strips. Refer to the quilt illustration on page 165.

7. Referring to the quilt illustration, sew the block rows and lattice strips together; press. <u>At this point the quilt center should measure 44-1/2 x 56 inches.</u>

Quilt Center Inner Border and Fence Border

Refer to **Binding and Diagonal Piecing** on page 221 for complete instructions with detailed illustrations.

NOTE: The yardage given allows for the borders to be cut on the crosswise grain.

Cutting

From **RED CHECK** cut
- 6—1-1/2 x 42-inch strips for quilt center inner border.
- 1—6-1/2 x 42-inch strip; from the strip cut 4—6-1/2-inch corner squares (to be set aside

and used in the fence border), and 4—2-1/2-inch corner squares.

From **BEIGE PRINT** cut
- 13—2-1/2 x 42-inch strips. Four of the strips will be used in strip sets, and from the remaining strips cut, 54—2-1/2 x 6-1/2-inch rectangles.

From **GREEN PRINT** cut
- 6—2-1/2 x 42-inch strips for the fence background.
- 8—2-1/2 x 42-inch strips for the fence background strip sets.
- 4—1-1/2 x 42-inch strips; from the strips cut 108—1-1/2-inch squares.

Attaching the Inner Borders

1. Measure the quilt from left to right through the center to determine the length of the top and bottom inner border strips. Cut 2, 1-1/2-inch wide RED CHECK strips to this measurement and pin them to the top and bottom of the quilt. Sew the strips to the quilt and press the seam allowances toward the border.

2. Measure the quilt from the top to bottom through the center, including the border strips just added, to determine the length of the side inner border strips. Cut 2, 1-1/2-inch wide RED CHECK strips to this measurement and pin them to the sides of the quilt. Sew the strips to the quilt and press the seam allowances toward the border.

3. Measure the quilt from left to right through the center to determine the length of the top and bottom GREEN PRINT fence background. Cut 2, 2-1/2-inch wide GREEN PRINT strips to this measurement and pin them to the top and bottom of the quilt. Sew the strips to the quilt and press the seam allowances toward the border.

4. Measure the quilt from the top to bottom through the center, including the seam allowances but not the fence background strips just added, to determine the length of the side fence background strips. Cut 2, 2-1/2-inch wide GREEN PRINT strips to this measurement and sew 2-1/2-inch RED CHECK corner squares to each end. Pin and sew the strips to the quilt and press the seam allowances toward the border.

Piecing and Attaching the Fence Border

1. Position a 1-1/2-inch GREEN PRINT square on the upper left corner of a 2-1/2 x 6-1/2-inch BEIGE PRINT rectangle. Draw a diagonal line on the GREEN PRINT square and stitch on the line. Trim the seam allowance to 1/4 inch; press. Repeat for the upper right corner of the BEIGE PRINT rectangle. <u>At this point each fence unit should measure 2-1/2 x 6-1/2-inches.</u>

Make 54

2. Sew a 2-1/2 x 42-inch GREEN PRINT strip to both sides of a 2-1/2 x 42-inch BEIGE PRINT strip; press. Make 4 strip sets. Cut the strip sets into segments.

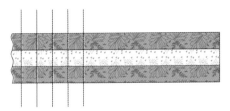

Crosscut 58, 2-1/2-inch wide segments

3. Referring to the quilt illustration, sew Step 1 and Step 2 segments together for the fence border strips; press. The top and bottom border strips each have 12, Step 1 segments and 13, Step 2 segments. Sew these border strips to the quilt; press.

4. The side fence border strips each have 15, Step 1 segments and 16, Step 2 segments. Add 6-1/2-inch wide RED CHECK corner squares to both ends of the side borders; press. Sew these borders to the quilt; press.

Outer Borders

Refer to **Binding and Diagonal Piecing** on page 221 for complete instructions with detailed illustrations.

NOTE: The yardage given allows for the borders to be cut on the crosswise grain.

Cutting

From **LARGE FLORAL** cut

- 10—6-1/2 x 42-inch strips for the outer border.
- 8—4-1/2 x 42-inch strips for the inner border.

From the **GREEN PRINT** cut
- 8—1-1/2 x 42-inch strips for the middle border.

Attaching the Outer Borders

1. Measure the quilt from left to right through the center to determine the length of the top and bottom inner border strips. Cut 2, 4-1/2-inch wide LARGE FLORAL strips to this measurement and pin them to the top and bottom of the quilt. Sew the strips to the quilt and press the seam allowances toward the border.

2. Measure the quilt from the top to bottom through the center, including the border strips just added, to determine the length of the side inner border strips. Cut 2, 4-1/2-inch wide LARGE FLORAL strips to this measurement and pin them to the sides of the quilt. Sew the strips to the quilt and press the seam allowances toward the border.

3. Measure the quilt from left to right through the center to determine the length of the top and bottom middle border strips. Cut 2, 1-1/2-inch wide GREEN PRINT strips to this measurement and pin them to the top and bottom of the quilt. Sew the strips to the quilt and press the seam allowances toward the border.

4. Measure the quilt from the top to bottom through the center, including the border strips just added, to determine the length of the side middle border strips. Cut 2, 1-1/2-inch wide GREEN PRINT strips to this length and sew them to the sides of the quilt. Press the seam allowances toward the border.

5. Measure the quilt from left to right through the center to determine the length of the top and bottom outer border strips. Cut 2, 6-1/2-inch wide LARGE FLORAL strips to this measurement and pin them to the top and bottom of the quilt. Sew the strips to the quilt and press the seam allowances toward the border.

6. Measure the quilt from top to bottom through the center, including the border strips just added to determine the length of the side outer border strips. Cut 2, 6-1/2-inch wide LARGE FLORAL

strips to this this measurement and pin them to the sides of the quilt. Sew the strips to the quilt and press the seam allowances toward the border.

Putting It All Together

Cut the 7-1/2 yard length of backing into thirds crosswise to make 3 lengths, 2-1/2 yards each.

Refer to **Finishing the Quilt** on page 221 for complete instructions.

Binding the Quilt

Refer to **Binding and Diagonal Piecing** on page 221 for complete instructions with detailed illustrations.

NOTE: The 2-3/4-inch strips will produce a 1/2-inch wide finished double binding. If you would like a wider or narrower binding, adjust the width of the strips.

Cutting

From **GREEN PLAID** cut
- 2-3/4-inch wide bias strips to make a strip approximately 380 inches long.

Sew the binding to the quilt using a 3/8-inch seam allowance.

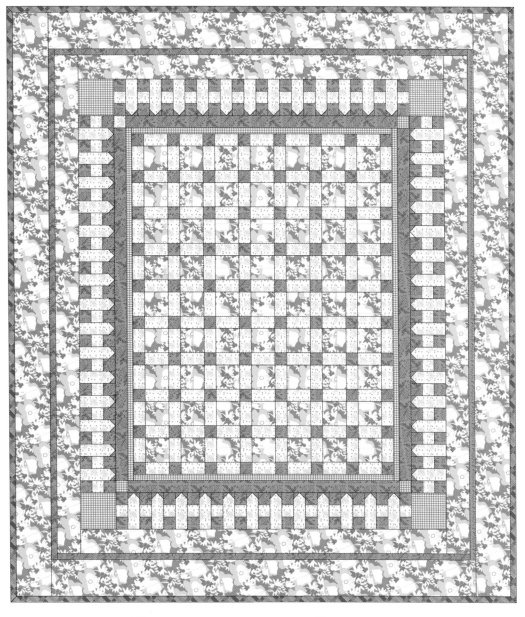

Courtyard Garden

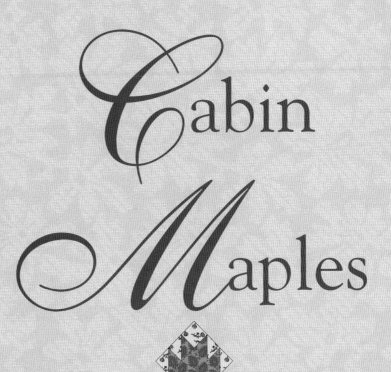

Cabin Maples

The lush, rich colors and
layers of pattern in Cabin
Maples are reminiscent of
the fall landscape with its
leaves of autumn that
tumble, twirl, and toss in
the wind before falling to the
ground in golden-hued piles.

Cabin Maples

Quilt measures 80 x 92 inches.
Block measures 9 inches square.

Fabric & Supplies

2-1/4 yards	**RED LEAF PRINT** for leaf blocks and Log Cabin center square
1-5/8 yards	**TAN SMALL LEAF PRINT** for leaf blocks
1/4 yard	**6 ASSORTED GREEN PRINTS** for Log Cabin strips
1/3 yard	**6 ASSORTED BROWN/RED PRINTS** for Log Cabin strips
1-3/8 yards	**BEIGE PRINT** for side and corner triangles
3/8 yard	**GREEN PRINT** for inner border
2-1/4 yards	**BROWN BERRY PRINT** for outer border
7/8 yard	**GREEN GRID** for binding
5-1/3 yards	Backing fabric
Quilt batting	84 x 96 inches

NOTE: read **Getting Started**, page 216, before beginning this project.

Leaf Blocks

Make 30 Blocks

Cutting

From **RED LEAF PRINT** cut
- 3—3-7/8 x 42-inch strips.
- 13—3-1/2 x 42-inch strips; from the strips cut 30—3-1/2 x 9-1/2-inch rectangles, and 30—3-1/2 x 6-1/2-inch rectangles.
- 5—1-1/4 x 42-inch strips; from the strips cut 30—1-1/4 x 6-inch strips.

From **TAN SMALL LEAF PRINT** cut
- 3—3-7/8 x 42-inch strips.
- 11—3-1/2 x 42-inch strips; from the strips cut 90—3-1/2-inch squares, and 30—3-1/2-inch squares. Cut the squares in half diagonally to make 60 triangles.

Piecing

1. With right sides together, layer the 3-7/8-inch wide RED LEAF PRINT and TAN SMALL LEAF PRINT strips in pairs. Press together, but do not sew. Cut the layered strips into 3-7/8-inch squares. Cut the layered squares in half diagonally to make 60 sets of triangles. Stitch 1/4-inch from the diagonal edge of each pair of triangles; press. <u>At this point each triangle-pieced square should measure 3-1/2-inches square.</u>

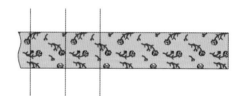

Crosscut 30 3-7/8-inch squares

Make 60 3-1/2-inch triangle-pieced squares

2. Sew the triangle-pieced squares together in pairs; press. Sew a 3-1/2-inch TAN SMALL LEAF PRINT square to the right edge of the triangle-pieced square unit. <u>At this point each section should measure 3-1/2 x 9-1/2 inches.</u>

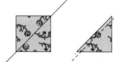

Make 30

3. Position a 3-1/2-inch TAN SMALL LEAF PRINT square on the corner of a 3-1/2 x 9-1/2-inch RED LEAF PRINT rectangle. Draw a diagonal line on the TAN SMALL LEAF PRINT square and stitch on the line. Trim the seam allowances to 1/4-inch; press. <u>At this point each section should measure 3-1/2 x 9-1/2 inches.</u>

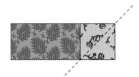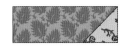

Make 30

4. Position a 3-1/2-inch TAN SMALL LEAF PRINT square on the corner of a 3-1/2 x 6-1/2-inch RED LEAF PRINT rectangle. Draw a diagonal line on the TAN SMALL LEAF PRINT square and stitch on the line. Trim the seam allowance to 1/4-inch; press.

Make 30

5. To make a stem unit, center a TAN SMALL LEAF PRINT triangle on a 1-1/4 x 6-inch RED LEAF PRINT strip and stitch a 1/4-inch seam. Center another TAN SMALL LEAF PRINT triangle on the opposite edge of the RED LEAF PRINT strip and stitch. Press the seam allowance toward the RED LEAF PRINT strip. Trim the stem unit so it measures 3-1/2 inches square.

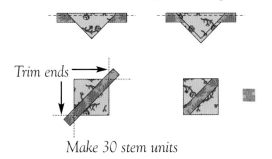

Make 30 stem units

6. Sew the stem unit to the left edge of the Step 4 unit; press. <u>At this point each section should measure 3-1/2 x 9-1/2-inches.</u>

Make 30

7. Referring to the block illustration, sew the Step 2, 3, and 6 sections together; press. <u>At this point each leaf block should measure 9-1/2-inches square.</u>

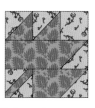

Make 30

Log Cabin Blocks

Make 20 Blocks

Cutting

From **RED LEAF PRINT** cut
- 2—3-1/2 x 42-inch strips.

From each of the 6 **ASSORTED GREEN PRINTS** cut
- 5—1-1/2 x 42-inch strips.

From each of the 6 **ASSORTED BROWN/RED PRINTS** cut
- 6—1-1/2 x 42-inch strips.

Piecing

NOTE: *You may vary the position of the ASSORTED GREEN PRINT strips from block to block or place them in the same position in each block. The same is true of the ASSORTED BROWN/RED PRINT strips. Follow Steps 1 through 5 to piece each of the 20 Log Cabin blocks.*

1. Aligning long edges, sew the 2, 3-1/2-inch wide RED LEAF PRINT strips and 2, of the 1-1/2-inch wide GREEN PRINT strips together in pairs; press. Make 2 strip sets. Cut the strip sets into segments.

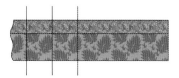

Crosscut 20, 3-1/2-inch wide segments

2. Stitch a different 1-1/2-inch wide GREEN PRINT strip to the two-piece unit. Press the seam allowance toward the strip. Trim the strip even with the edges of the two-piece unit.

3. Turn the unit a quarter turn to the left. Stitch a 1-1/2-inch wide BROWN/RED PRINT strip to the unit. Press and trim the strip even with the edges of the unit.

4. Turn the unit a quarter turn to the left. Stitch a different 1-1/2-inch wide BROWN/RED PRINT strip to the unit. Press and trim the strip even with the edges of the unit.

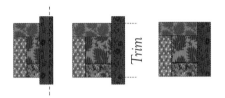

5. Referring to the block illustration, continue this process by adding 1-1/2-inch wide GREEN PRINT strips and BROWN/RED PRINT strips to complete the Log Cabin block. Press each seam allowance toward the strip just added, and trim each strip before adding the next. Each Log Cabin block should measure 9-1/2 inches square when completed. Adjust the seam allowances if needed.

Make 20

Quilt Center

NOTE: *The side and corner triangles are larger than necessary and will be trimmed before the borders are added.*

Cutting

From **BEIGE PRINT** cut
- 3—15 x 42-inch strips; from the strips cut 5—15-inch squares. Cut the squares diagonally into quarters for 20 triangles. You will be using only 18 for side triangles.
  2—8-1/2-inch squares. Cut the squares in half diagonally for 4 corner triangles.

Quilt Center Assembly

1. Referring to the quilt illustration for block placement, sew the leaf blocks, Log Cabin blocks, and BEIGE PRINT side triangles together in diagonal rows to make 10 block rows. Press the seam allowances in alternating directions by rows so the seams will fit snugly together with less bulk.

2. Pin the rows and the block intersections and sew the rows together. Press the seam allowances in one direction.

3. Sew the BEIGE PRINT corner triangles to the quilt center; press.

4. Trim away excess fabric from side and corner triangles taking care to allow a 1/4-inch seam allowance beyond the corners of each block.

Refer to page 218 for **Trimming Side and Corner Triangles**.

Borders

Refer to **Binding and Diagonal Piecing** on page 221 for complete instructions with detailed illustrations.

NOTE: *The yardage given allows for the border strips to be cut on the crosswise grain.*

Cutting

From **GREEN PRINT** cut
- 8—1-1/2 x 42-inch strips for the inner border.

From **BROWN BERRY PRINT**
- 10—7-1/2 x 42-inch strips for the outer border.

Attaching the Borders

1. Measure the quilt from left to right through the center to determine the length of the top and bottom inner border strips. Cut 2, 1-1/2-inch wide GREEN PRINT strips to this measurement and pin them to the top and bottom of the quilt. Sew the strips to the quilt and press the seam allowances toward the border.

2. Measure the quilt from the top to bottom through the center, including the border strips just added, to determine the length of the side inner border strips. Cut 2, 1-1/2-inch wide GREEN PRINT strips to this measurement and

pin them to the sides of the quilt. Sew the strips to the quilt and press the seam allowances toward the border.

3. Measure the quilt from left to right through the center to determine the length of the top and bottom outer border strips. Cut 2, 7-1/2-inch wide BROWN BERRY PRINT strips to this measurement and pin them to the top and bottom of the quilt. Sew the strips to the quilt and press the seam allowances toward the border.

4. Measure the quilt from the top to bottom through the center, including the border strips just added, to determine the length of the side outer border strips. Cut 2, 7-1/2-inch wide BROWN BERRY PRINT strips to this measurement and pin them to the sides of the quilt. Sew the strips to the quilt and press the seam allowances toward the border.

Putting It All Together

Cut the 5-1/3 yard length of backing fabric in half crosswise to make 2, 2-2/3 yard lengths.

Refer to **Finishing the Quilt** on page 221 for complete instructions.

Binding the Quilt

Refer to **Binding and Diagonal Piecing** on page 221 for complete instructions with detailed illustrations.

NOTE: The 2-3/4-inch strips will produce a 1/2-inch wide finished double binding. If you would like a wider or narrower binding, adjust the width of the strips.

Cutting

From **GREEN GRID** cut
*   10—2-3/4 x 42-inch strips.

Sew the binding to the quilt using a 3/8-inch seam allowance.

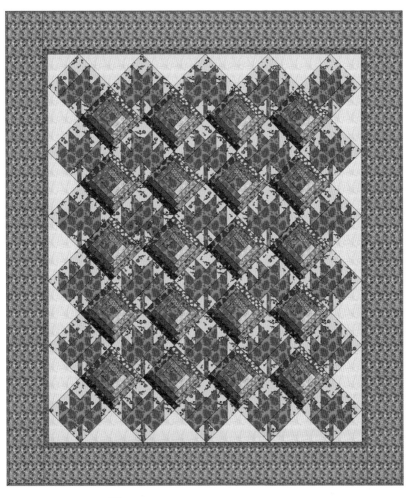

Cabin Maples

Party Mix

For the beginner,
surprisingly simple blocks
with the antique look
of old-fashioned patchwork
and straight forward
borders, are a great mix!
(For an alternate color
option, see page 176.)

Party Mix

Quilt measures 74 x 86 inches.
Block measures 6 inches square.

Fabric & Supplies

1/2 yard	**9 COORDINATING DARK PRINTS** for blocks
5/8 yard	**TAN PRINT #1** for blocks
5/8 yard	**TAN PRINT #2** for blocks
2/3 yard	**CHESTNUT PRINT** for inner border and corner squares
5/8 yard	**BROWN PRINT** for middle border
1-3/4 yards	**RED FLORAL** for outer border
3/4 yard	**BLUE PRINT** for binding
5 yards	Backing fabric
Quilt batting	78 x 90 inches

NOTE: read **Getting Started**,
page 216, before beginning this project.

Pieced Blocks

Make 99 Blocks

Cutting

From each of the 9 **DARK PRINTS** cut
- 2—6-1/2 x 42-inch strips; from the strips cut 11—6-1/2-inch squares for 99 DARK PRINT squares.

From **TAN PRINT #1** cut
- 7—2-1/2 x 42-inch strips; from the strips cut 100—2-1/2-inch squares.

From **TAN PRINT #2** cut
- 7—2-1/2 x 42-inch strips; from the strips cut 98—2-1/2-inch squares.

Piecing

1. Position 2-1/2-inch TAN PRINT #1 squares on 2 opposite corners of a 6-1/2-inch DARK PRINT square. Draw a diagonal line on each TAN PRINT #1 square, and stitch on the line. Trim the seam allowances to 1/4-inch; press.

Make 50

2. Position 2-1/2-inch TAN PRINT #2 squares on 2 opposite corners of a 6-1/2-inch DARK PRINT square. Draw a diagonal line on each TAN PRINT #2 square, and stitch on the line. Trim the seam allowances to 1/4-inch; press.

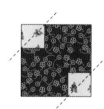

Make 49

Quilt Center

1. Referring to the quilt illustration for block placement, sew the blocks together in 11 horizontal rows of 9 blocks each. Press the

seam allowances in alternating directions by rows so the seams will fit snugly together with less bulk.

2. Pin the rows at the block intersections, and sew the rows together. Press the seam allowances in one direction.

Borders

Refer to **Binding and Diagonal Piecing** on page 221 for complete instructions with detailed illustrations.

NOTE: *The yardage given allows for the border strips to be cut on the crosswise grain.*

Cutting

From **CHESTNUT PRINT** cut
- 7—2-1/2 x 42-inch strips for the inner border.
- 4—2-1/2-inch corner squares.

From **BROWN PRINT** cut
- 7—2-1/2 x 42-inch strips for the middle border.

From **RED FLORAL** cut
- 9—6-1/2 x 42-inch strips for the outer border.

Attaching the Borders

1. Measure the quilt from left to right through the center to determine the length of the top and bottom inner border strips. Cut 2, 2-1/2-inch wide CHESTNUT PRINT strips to this measurement and pin them to the top and bottom of the quilt. Sew the strips to the quilt and press the seam allowances toward the border.

2. Measure the quilt from the top to bottom through the center, including the border strips just added, to determine the length of the side inner border strips. Cut 2, 2-1/2-inch wide CHESTNUT PRINT strips to this measurement and pin them to the sides of the quilt. Sew the strips to the quilt and press the seam allowances toward the border.

3. Measure the quilt from left to right through the center to determine the length of the top and bottom middle border strips. Cut 2, 2-1/2-inch wide BROWN PRINT strips to this measurement and pin them to the top and bottom of the quilt. Sew the strips to the quilt and press the seam allowances toward the border.

4. Measure the quilt from the top to bottom through the center, including the seam allowances but not the border strips just added, to determine the length of the side middle border strips. Cut 2, 2-1/2-inch wide BROWN PRINT strips to this measurement and sew 2-1/2-inch CHESTNUT PRINT corner squares to each end. Pin strips to the sides of the quilt. Sew the strips to the quilt and press the seam allowances toward the border.

5. Measure the quilt from left to right through the center to determine the length of the top and bottom outer border strips. Cut 2, 6-1/2-inch wide RED FLORAL strips to this measurement and pin them to the top and bottom of the quilt. Sew the strips to the quilt and press the seam allowances toward the border.

6. Measure the quilt from the top to bottom through the center, including the border strips just added, to determine the length of the side outer border strips. Cut 2, 6-1/2-inch wide RED FLORAL strips to this measurement and pin them to the sides of the quilt. Sew the strips to the quilt and press the seam allowances toward the border.

Putting It All Together

Cut the 5 yard length of backing fabric in half to make 2, 2-1/2 yard lengths.

Refer to **Finishing the Quilt** on page 221 for complete instructions.

Binding

Refer to **Binding and Diagonal Piecing** on page 221 for complete instructions with detailed illustrations.

NOTE:*The 2-3/4-inch strips will produce a 1/2-inch wide finished double binding. If you would like a wider or narrower binding, adjust the width of the strips.*

Cutting

From **BLUE PRINT** cut
- 9—2-3/4 x 42-inch strips.

Sew the binding to the quilt using a 3/8-inch seam allowance.

Alternate Color Option

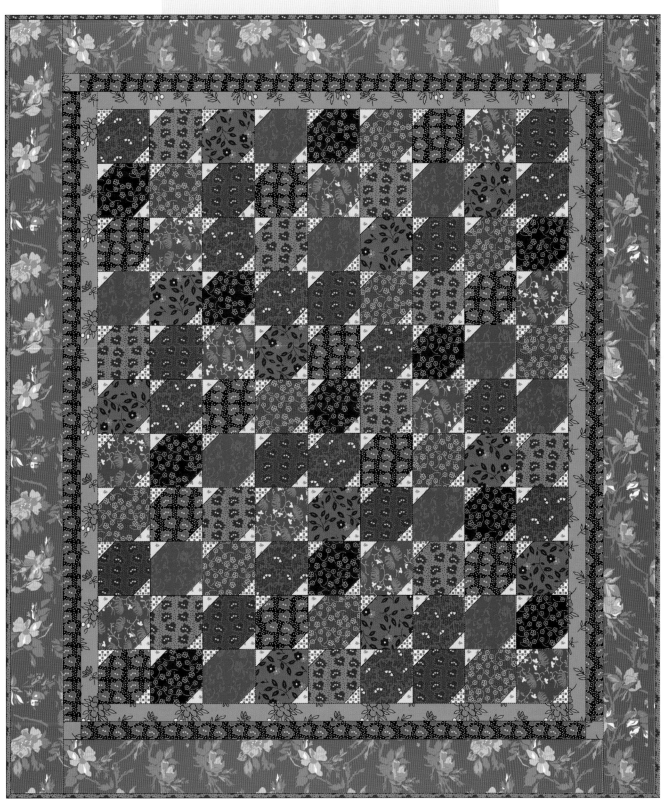

Party Mix

Garden Scape

As warm as it is
inviting, this flannel
log cabin features blocks with
traditional Log Cabin piecing—
one side is light and one side
is dark. The result yields a
stunning block setting of light
and dark alternating-on-point
designs, shown here
and on the following page.

Garden Scape

Quilt measures 64 x 80 inches.
Block measures 8 inches square.

If using flannel, refer to **Helpful Hints for Sewing with Flannel** *on page 219.*

Fabric & Supplies

1/2 yard	**5 LIGHT** to **MEDIUM PRINTS** for Log Cabin strips
1 yard	**5 DARK PRINTS** for Log Cabin strips and pieced border
1/2 yard	**BROWN DIAGONAL PRINT** for center squares
1-1/8 yards	**TAN PRINT** for pieced border
7/8 yard	**BROWN DIAGONAL PRINT** for binding
4-2/3 yards	Backing fabric
Quilt batting	68 x 84 inches

NOTE: read **Getting Started**, *page 216, before beginning this project.*

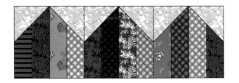

Log Cabin Blocks

Make 48 Blocks from LIGHT to MEDIUM and DARK PRINTS

Make 4 Blocks from DARK PRINTS

Cutting

From 5 **LIGHT to MEDIUM PRINTS** cut
- approximately 46—1-1/2 x 42-inch strips.

From 5 **DARK PRINTS** cut
- approximately 56—1-1/2 x 42-inch strips.

From **BROWN DIAGONAL PRINT** cut
- 4—2-1/2 x 42-inch strips; from the strips cut 52—2-1/2-inch squares.

Piecing

1. Sew a 1-1/2-inch wide LIGHT PRINT strip to a 2-1/2-inch BROWN DIAGONAL PRINT square. Press the seam allowance toward the strip just added. Trim the strip even with the edges of the center square, creating a two-piece unit.

2. Turn the unit to the left a quarter turn. Sew a 1-1/2-inch wide LIGHT PRINT strip to the two-piece unit. Press and trim the strip even with the edges of the two-piece unit.

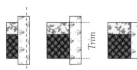

3. Turn the unit to the left a quarter turn. Sew a 1-1/2-inch wide DARK PRINT strip to the three-piece unit. Press and trim the strip even with the edges of the three-piece unit. Turn the unit again to the left; add another DARK PRINT strip; press and trim.

4. Continue adding LIGHT PRINT and DARK PRINT strips, referring to the Log Cabin block illustration for color placement. Press each seam allowance toward the strip just added, and trim each strip before adding the next. <u>At this point, the Log Cabin block should measure 8-1/2-inches square.</u>

Make 48   *Make 4*

5. Repeat steps 1 through 4 to make 48 LIGHT to MEDIUM and DARK PRINT Log Cabin blocks. Make 4 corner Log Cabin blocks in the same manner, except use DARK PRINT strips.

Quilt Center

1. Lay out the Log Cabin blocks, referring to the quilt illustration for color placement. Sew the blocks together in 8 horizontal rows of 6 blocks each. Press the seam allowances in alternating directions by rows so the seams will fit snugly. Sew the rows together; press.

2. Pin the rows at the block intersections, and sew the rows together. Press the seam allowances in one direction.

Border

Cutting

From 5 **DARK PRINTS** cut
- 112—2-1/2 x 8-1/2-inch rectangles.

From **TAN PRINT** cut
- 7—4-1/2 x 42-inch strips; from the strips cut 56—4-1/2-inch squares.

Piecing

1. Sew the 2-1/2 x 8-1/2-inch DARK PRINT rectangles together in pairs; press.

2. Position a 4-1/2-inch TAN PRINT square on the Step 1 pair. Draw a diagonal line on the TAN PRINT square and stitch on the line. Trim the seam; press.

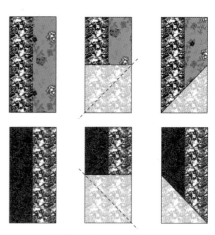

Make 28 of each.

3. Sew the Step 2 units together in pairs; press.

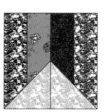

Make 28

4. Sew 6, Step 3 units together for the top border and for the bottom border; press. Sew the pieced borders to the quilt; press.

5. Sew 8, Step 3 units together for each side border, and press. Add a dark Log Cabin block to each end of the borders; and press. Sew the pieced borders to the quilt; press.

Putting It All Together

Cut the 4-2/3 yard length of backing fabric in half crosswise to make 2, 2-1/3-yard lengths.

Refer to **Finishing The Quilt** on page 221 for complete instructions.

Binding the Quilt

Refer to **Binding and Diagonal Piecing** on page 221 for complete instructions with detailed illustrations.

NOTE: The 2-3/4-inch strips will produce a 1/2-inch wide finished double binding. If you would like a wider or narrower binding, adjust the width of the strips.

Sew the binding to the quilt using a 3/8-inch seam allowance.

Garden Scape

Crossroads

Blocks set on point create
an unusual basket-weave
effect in this striking
variation of the traditional
Split Rail Fence quilt.
The large pieces lend
themselves well to flannel.

Crossroads

Quilt measures 77 x 91 inches.
Block measures 10 inches square.

Fabric & Supplies

3-3/8 yards	**LARGE ROSE FLORAL** for blocks and outer border
2/3 yard	**GREEN FLORAL** for blocks
1-1/4 yards	**GREEN PRINT #1** for blocks and inner border
1 yard	**EGGPLANT PRINT** for blocks
2/3 yard	**BEIGE PRINT #1** for blocks
3/8 yard	**BEIGE PRINT #2** for blocks
3/8 yard	**TAN PRINT** for blocks
3/8 yard	**GREEN PRINT #2** for blocks
1-1/2 yards	**BEIGE PRINT #3** for side and corner triangles
7/8 yard	**GREEN FLORAL** for binding
5-1/4 yards	Backing fabric
Quilt batting	81 x 95 inches

*NOTE: read **Getting Started**, page 216, before beginning this project.*

Block A

Make 20 Blocks

Cutting

From **LARGE ROSE FLORAL, GREEN FLORAL, EGGPLANT, BEIGE #1,** and **GREEN #1 PRINTS** cut
- 7—2-1/2 x 42-inch strips from each of these fabrics.

Piecing

Aligning long edges, sew one of each of the above strips together to form a strip set; press. Make 7 strip sets. Cut the strip sets into segments. <u>At this point each block should measure 10-1/2 inches square.</u>

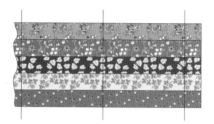

Crosscut 20, 10-1/2 inch squares   *Block A*

Block B

Make 12 Blocks

Cutting

From **GREEN #2, BEIGE #2, LARGE ROSE FLORAL, TAN,** and **EGGPLANT PRINTS** cut
- 4—2-1/2 x 42-inch strips from each of these fabrics.

Piecing

Aligning long edges, sew one of each of the above strips together to form a strip set; press. Make 4 strip sets. Cut the strip sets into segments. <u>At this point each block should measure 10-1/2 inches square.</u>

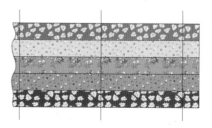 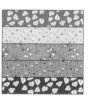

Crosscut 12, 10-1/2 inch squares   *Block B*

Quilt Center

NOTE: The side and corner triangles are larger than necessary and will be trimmed before the borders are added.

Cutting

From **BEIGE PRINT #3** cut
- 2—16-1/2 x 42-inch strips; from the strip cut 4—16-1/2-inch squares. Cut the squares diagonally into quarters for a total of 16 triangles. You will be using only 14 for side triangles.
- 1—10-1/2x 42-inch strip; from the strip cut 2—10-1/2-inch squares. Cut the squares in half diagonally for 4 corner triangles.

Assembling the Quilt Center

1. Refer to the quilt illustration and sew together the pieced blocks and side triangles in diagonal rows. Press the seam allowances in alternating directions by rows so the seams will fit snugly together with less bulk.

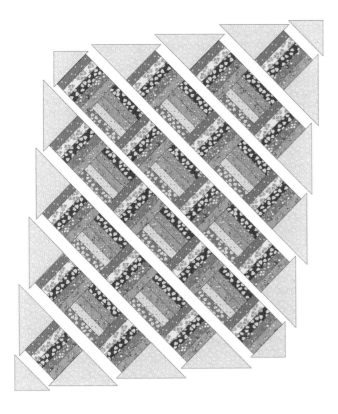

2. Pin the rows at the block intersections and sew the rows together. Press the seam allowances in one direction.

3. Sew the corner triangles to the quilt; press.

4. Trim away the excess fabric from the side and corner triangles, taking care to allow a 1/4-inch seam allowance beyond the corners of each block.

Refer to page 218 for **Trimming Side and Corner Triangles**.

Borders

Refer to **Binding and Diagonal Piecing** on page 221 for complete instructions with detailed illustrations.

NOTE: The yardage given allows for the border strips to be cut on the crosswise grain.

Cutting

From **GREEN PRINT #1** cut
- 7—2-1/2 x 42-inch inner border strips.

From **LARGE ROSE FLORAL** cut
- 10—8-1/2 x 42-inch outer border strips.

Attaching the Borders

1. Measure the quilt from left to right through the center to determine the length of the top and bottom inner border strips. Cut 2, 2-1/2-inch wide GREEN PRINT #1 strips to this measurement and pin them to the top and bottom of the quilt. Sew the strips to the quilt and press the seam allowances toward the border.

2. Measure the quilt from the top to bottom through the center, including the border strips just added, to determine the length of the side inner border strips. Cut 2, 2-1/2-inch wide GREEN PRINT #1 strips to this measurement and pin them to the sides of the quilt. Sew the strips to the quilt and press the seam allowances toward the border.

3. Measure the quilt from left to right through the center to determine the length of the top and bottom outer border strips. Cut 2, 8-1/2-inch wide LARGE ROSE FLORAL strips to this measurement and pin them to the top and bottom of the quilt. Sew the strips to the quilt and press the seam allowances toward the border.

4. Measure the quilt from top to bottom through the center, including the border strips just added to determine the length of the side outer border strips. Cut 2, 8-1/2-inch wide LARGE ROSE FLORAL strips to this measurement and pin them to the sides of the quilt. Sew the strips to the quilt and press the seam allowances toward the border.

Putting It All Together

Cut the 5-1/4 yard length of backing fabric in half crosswise to make 2, 2-5/8 yard lengths.

Refer to **Finishing the Quilt** on page 221 for complete instructions.

Binding

Refer to **Binding and Diagonal Piecing** on page 221 for complete instructions with detailed illustrations.

NOTE: The 2-3/4-inch strips will produce a 1/2-inch wide finished double binding. If you would like a wider or narrower binding, adjust the width of the strips.

Cutting

From **GREEN FLORAL** cut
  • 9—3 x 42-inch strips.

Sew the binding to the quilt using a 3/8-inch seam allowance.

Crossroads

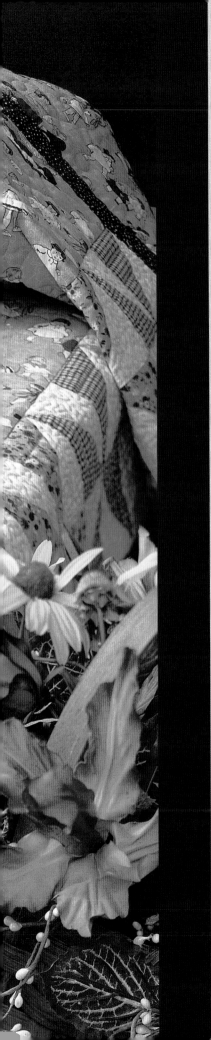

Party
Pinwheels

Playful pinwheels
provide contrast for
large vertical strips
showcasing novelty prints—
perfect for a child's bedroom!

Party Pinwheels

Quilt measures 80 x 96 inches.
Block measures 8 inches square.

Fabric & Supplies

7/8 yard	**GOLD PRINT** for pinwheel blocks
7/8 yard	**BLUE/GREEN CHECK** for pinwheel blocks
2/3 yard	**GREEN PRINT** for pinwheel blocks
2-1/8 yards	**BEIGE PRINT** for pinwheel blocks
3-5/8 yards	**LARGE GREEN PRINT** for lattice and outer border
2/3 yard	**RED PRINT** for inner border
7/8 yard	**BLUE/RED/BEIGE DIAGONAL PRINT** for binding
5-1/2 yards	Backing fabric
Quilt batting	84 x 100 inches

NOTE: read **Getting Started**,
page 216, before beginning this project.

Pinwheel Blocks

Make 17 A Blocks
Make 17 B Blocks
Make 16 C Blocks

Cutting

From **GOLD PRINT** cut
- 5—4-7/8 x 42-inch strips.

From **BLUE/GREEN CHECK** cut
- 5—4-7/8 x 42-inch strips.

From **GREEN PRINT** cut
- 4—4-7/8 x 42-inch strips.

From **BEIGE PRINT** cut
- 14—4-7/8 x 42-inch strips.

Piecing

1. With right sides together, layer the 4-7/8 x 42-inch GOLD PRINT strips and 5 BEIGE PRINT strips in pairs. Press together, but do not sew. Cut the layered strips into squares. Cut the layered squares in half diagonally to make 68 sets of triangles. Stitch 1/4-inch from the diagonal edge of each pair of triangles; press. <u>At this point each triangle-pieced square should measure 4-1/2 inches square.</u>

Crosscut 34, 4-7/8-inch squares

Make 68, 4-1/2-inch triangle-pieced squares

2. Sew the triangle-pieced squares together in pairs; press. Sew the pairs together to form the pinwheel block. <u>At this point each pinwheel block should measure 8-1/2 inches square.</u>

Make 34

Make 17

Block A

3. Following Steps 1 and 2, make 17 BLUE/GREEN CHECK and BEIGE PRINT pinwheel blocks. <u>At this point each pinwheel block should measure 8-1/2-inches square.</u>

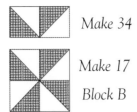

Make 34

Make 17

Block B

4. With right sides together, layer the 4-7/8 x 42-inch GREEN PRINT strips and 4 of the BEIGE PRINT strips in pairs. Following Steps 1 and 2, make 16 GREEN PRINT and BEIGE PRINT pinwheel blocks. <u>At this point each pinwheel block should measure 8-1/2 inches square.</u>

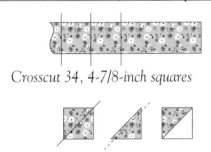

Crosscut 34, 4-7/8-inch squares

Make 68, 4-1/2-inch triangle-pieced squares

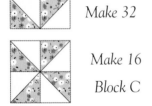

Make 32

Make 16

Block C

Quilt Center and Borders

Refer to **Binding and Diagonal Piecing** on page 221 for complete instructions with detailed illustrations.

NOTE: The yardage given allows for the **LARGE GREEN PRINT** *vertical lattice strips and the side border strips to be cut on the lengthwise grain. The yardage given allows for the* **LARGE GREEN PRINT** *top and bottom outer border stirps and the* **RED PRINT** *inner border strips to be cut on the crosswise grain.*

Cutting

From **LARGE GREEN PRINT** cut
- 4—6-1/2 x 42-inch top and bottom outer border strips on the crosswise grain.
- 4—6-1/2 x 83-inch vertical lattice strips on the lengthwise grain.
- 2—6-1/2 x 100-inch side outer border strips on the lengthwise grain.

From **RED PRINT** cut
- 8—2-1/2 x 42-inch inner border strips.

Quilt Center Assembly

1. Referring to the quilt illustration for block placement, sew the A, B, and C blocks together in 5 vertical rows of 10 blocks each. Press the seam allowances in one direction. <u>At this point each block row should measure 8-1/2 x 80-1/2 inches.</u>

2. Cut the 4, 6-1/2 x 83-inch LARGE GREEN PRINT vertical lattice strips to 80-1/2 inches long or to the measurement of your block rows. Pin together the 5 block rows and the 4 LARGE GREEN PRINT vertical lattice strips. Sew the strips together; press.

Attaching the Borders

1. Measure the quilt from left to right through the center to determine the length of the top and bottom inner border strips. Cut 2, 2-1/2-inch wide RED PRINT strips to this measurement and pin them to the top and bottom of the quilt. Sew the strips to the quilt and press the seam allowances toward the border.

2. Measure the quilt from the top to bottom through the center, including the border strips just added, to determine the length of the side inner border strips. Cut 2, 2-1/2-inch wide RED PRINT strips to this measurement and pin them to the sides of the quilt. Sew the strips to the quilt and press the seam allowances toward the border.

3. Measure the quilt from left to right through the center to determine the length of the top and bottom outer border strips. Cut 2, 6-1/2-inch wide LARGE GREEN PRINT strips to this measurement and pin them to the top and bottom of the quilt. Sew the strips to the quilt and press the seam allowances toward the border.

4. Measure the quilt from top to bottom through the center, including the border strips just added to determine the length of the side outer border strips. Cut 2, 6-1/2 x 100-inch LARGE GREEN PRINT strips to this measurement and pin them

to the sides of the quilt. Sew the strips to the quilt and press the seam allowances toward the border.

Putting It All Together

Cut the 5-1/2-yard length of backing fabric in half crosswise to make 2, 2-3/4-yard lengths.

Refer to **Finishing the Quilt** on page 221 for complete instructions.

Binding the Quilt

Refer to **Binding and Diagonal Piecing** on page 221 for complete instructions with detailed illustrations.

NOTE: *The 2-3/4-inch strips will produce a 1/2-inch wide finished double binding. If you would like a wider or narrower binding, adjust the width of the strips.*

Cutting

From **BLUE/RED/BEIGE DIAGONAL PRINT** cut
*   9—2-3/4 x 42-inch strips.

Sew the binding to the quilt using a 3/8-inch seam allowance.

Party Pinwheels

Fireside Strippy

The flannel version of party pinwheels aptly demonstrates the power of contrasting colors. Changing from light pastels to dark plaids transforms the pattern into a handsome, country casual comforter.

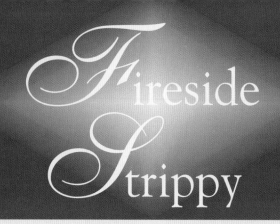

Fireside Strippy

Quilt measures 80 x 96 inches.
Block measures 8 inches square.

Fabric & Supplies

3-3/4 yards	**RED PLAID** for pinwheel blocks and outer border (cut lengthwise)
7/8 yard	**GREEN/TAN PLAID** for pinwheel blocks
2/3 yard	**GREEN/RED PLAID** for pinwheel blocks
2-1/8 yards	**BEIGE PLAID** for pinwheel background
2-1/2 yards	**RED/GREEN PLAID** for lattice (cut lengthwise)
3/4 yard	**DARK GREEN PLAID** for inner border
7/8 yard	**BLACK/RED/TAN PLAID** for binding (cut on bias)
5-1/2 yards	Backing fabric
Quilt batting	84 x 100 inches

NOTE: read **Getting Started**,
page 216, before beginning this project.

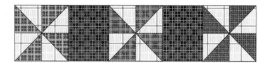

Pinwheel Blocks

Make 17 A Blocks
Make 17 B Blocks
Make 16 C Blocks

Cutting

From **RED PLAID** cut
- 5—4-7/8 x 42-inch strips.

From **GREEN/TAN PLAID** cut
- 5—4-7/8 x 42-inch strips.

From **GREEN/RED PLAID** cut
- 4—4-7/8 x 42-inch strips.

From **BEIGE PLAID** cut
- 14—4-7/8 x 42-inch strips.

Piecing

1. With right sides together, layer the 4-7/8 x 42-inch RED PLAID strips and 5 of the BEIGE PLAID strips in pairs. Press together, but do not sew. Cut the layered strips into squares. Cut the layered squares in half diagonally to make 68 sets of triangles. Stitch 1/4-inch from the diagonal edge of each pair of triangles; press. <u>At this point each triangle-pieced square should measure 4-1/2 inches square.</u>

Crosscut 34, 4-7/8-inch squares

Make 68, 4-1/2-inch triangle-pieced squares

2. Sew the triangle-pieced squares together in pairs; press. Sew the pairs together to form the pinwheel block. <u>At this time each pinwheel Block A should measure 8-1/2 inches square.</u>

 Make 34

 Make 17

Block A

3. Following Steps 1 and 2, make 17 GREEN/TAN PLAID and BEIGE PLAID pinwheel blocks. <u>At this point each pinwheel Block B should measure 8-1/2-inches square.</u>

 Make 34

 Make 17

Block B

4. With right sides together, layer the 4-7/8 x 42-inch GREEN/RED PLAID strips and 4 of the BEIGE PLAID strips in pairs. Following Steps 1 and 2, make 16 GREEN/RED PLAID and BEIGE PLAID pinwheel blocks. <u>At this point each pinwheel Block C should measure 8-1/2 inches square.</u>

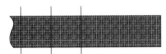

Crosscut 32, 4-7/8-inch squares

Make 64, 4-1/2-inch triangle-pieced squares

 Make 32

 Make 16

Block C

Quilt Center and Borders

Refer to **Binding and Diagonal Piecing** on page 221 for complete instructions with detailed illustrations.

NOTE: The yardage given allows for the **RED/GREEN PLAID** *vertical lattice strips and the* **RED PLAID** *outer border strips to be cut on the lengthwise grain. Cutting the strips on the lengthwise grain will eliminate the need for piecing and matching the plaid strips. The yardage given allows for the* **DARK GREEN PLAID** *inner border strips to be cut on the crosswise grain since the piecing will not be as noticeable.*

Cutting

From **RED/GREEN PLAID** cut

- 4—6-1/2 x 83-inch vertical lattice strips on the lengthwise grain.

From **DARK GREEN PLAID** cut

- 8—2-1/2 x 42-inch inner border strips on the crosswise grain.

From **RED PLAID** cut

- 2—6-1/2 x 100-inch side outer border strips on the lengthwise grain.
- 2—6-1/2 x 72-inch top and bottom outer border strips on the lengthwise grain.

Quilt Center Assembly

1. Referring to the quilt illustration for block placement, sew the A, B, and C blocks together in 5 vertical rows of 10 blocks each. Press the seam allowances in one direction. <u>At this point each block row should measure 8-1/2 x 80-1/2-inches.</u>

2. Cut the 4, 6-1/2 x 83-inch RED/GREEN PLAID vertical lattice strips to 80-1/2 inches long or to the measurement of your block rows. Pin together the 5 block rows and the 4, 6-1/2-inch wide RED/GREEN PLAID vertical lattice strips. Sew the strips together; press.

Attaching the Borders

1. Measure the quilt from left to right through the center to determine the length of the top and bottom inner border strips. Cut 2, 2-1/2-inch wide DARK GREEN PLAID strips to this measurement and pin them to the top and bottom of the quilt. Sew the strips to the quilt and press the seam allowances toward the border.

2. Measure the quilt from the top to bottom through the center, including the border strips just added, to determine the length of the side inner border strips. Cut 2, 2-1/2-inch wide DARK GREEN PLAID strips to this measurement and pin them to the sides of the quilt. Sew the strips to the quilt and press the seam allowances toward the border.

3. Measure the quilt from left to right through the center to determine the length of the top and bottom outer border strips. Cut 2, 6-1/2 x 72-inch RED PLAID strips to this measurement and pin them to the top and bottom of the quilt. Sew the strips to the quilt and press the seam allowances toward the border.

4. Measure the quilt from top to bottom through the center, including the border strips just added to determine the length of the side outer border strips. Cut 2, 6-1/2 x 100-inch RED PLAID strips to this measurement and pin them to the sides of the quilt. Sew the strips to the quilt and press the seam allowances toward the border.

Putting It All Together

Cut the 5-1/2-yard length of backing fabric in half crosswise to make 2, 2-3/4-yard lengths.

Refer to **Finishing the Quilt** on page 221 for complete instructions.

Binding the Quilt

Refer to **Binding and Diagonal Piecing** on page 221 for complete instructions with detailed illustrations.

NOTE: The 3-inch strips will produce a 1/2-inch wide finished double binding. If you would like a wider or narrower binding, adjust the width of the strips.

Cutting

From **BLACK/RED/TAN PLAID** cut
- 3-inch wide bias strips to make a strip approximately 370 inches long.

Sew the binding to the quilt using a 3/8-inch seam allowance.

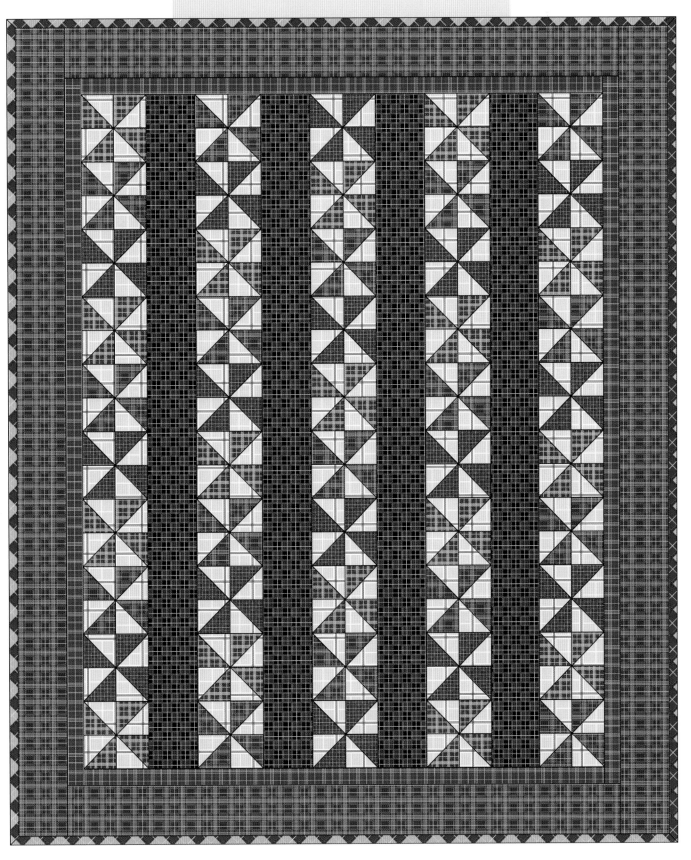

Fireside Strippy

September Stars

Spending an evening under
the stars has never been easier!
Snuggle up in a bed-size
quilt composed of numerous
background blocks that
shadow the star points providing
subtle, visual texture—soft,
yet noticeable—creating a
harmonious framework
for the stars.

September Stars

Quilt measures 81 x 93 inches.
Block measures 9 inches square.

Fabric & Supplies

3-5/8 yards	**RED PRINT** for star blocks and border
1-7/8 yards	**CREAM PRINT** for star blocks
1 yard	**BEIGE GRID** for star blocks
1-1/4 yards	**TAN BERRY PRINT** for star blocks and pieced lattice
1-2/3 yards	**MEDIUM GREEN PRINT** for pieced lattice
1/2 yard	**GREEN PRINT** for lattice posts
7/8 yard	**GREEN PRINT** for binding
7-1/8 yards	Backing fabric
Quilt batting	85 x 97 inches

NOTE: read **Getting Started**, page 216, before beginning this project.

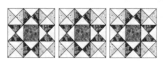

Star Blocks

Make 30 Blocks

Cutting

From **RED PRINT** cut
- 7—4-1/4 x 42-inch strips; from the strips cut 60—4-1/4-inch squares. Cut the squares diagonally into quarters, forming 240 triangles.

From **CREAM PRINT** cut
- 14—4-1/4 x 42-inch strips; from the strips cut 120—4-1/4-inch squares. Cut the squares diagonally into quarters, forming 480 triangles.

From **BEIGE GRID** cut
- 7—4-1/4 x 42-inch strips; from the strips cut 60—4-1/4-inch squares. Cut the squares diagonally into quarters, forming 240 triangles.

From **TAN BERRY PRINT** cut
- 3—3-1/2 x 42-inch strips; from the strips cut 30—3-1/2-inch squares.

Piecing

1. Layer a RED PRINT triangle on a CREAM PRINT triangle. Stitch along the bias edge as shown, being careful not to stretch the triangles. Press the seam allowance toward the RED PRINT triangle. Make sure to sew with the RED PRINT fabric on top, and stitch along the same bias edge of each triangle set. Repeat for all remaining RED PRINT triangles and 239 CREAM PRINT triangles. Sew the triangle units together in pairs; press. <u>At this point each triangle block should measure 3-1/2-inches square.</u>

Bias edge

Make 240 triangle units   *Make 120 triangle blocks*

2. Layer a BEIGE GRID triangle on a CREAM PRINT triangle. Stitch along the bias edge as shown, being careful not to stretch the triangles. Press the seam allowance toward

the BEIGE GRID triangle. Make sure to sew with the BEIGE GRID fabric on top, and stitch along the same bias edge of each triangle set. Repeat for the remaining CREAM PRINT and BEIGE GRID triangles. Sew the triangle units together in pairs; press. <u>At this point each triangle block should measure 3-1/2-inches square.</u>

Make 240
triangle units   Make 120
triangle blocks

3. Referring to the diagram, sew Step 1 triangle blocks to both sides of a 3-1/2-inch TAN BERRY PRINT square. Press the seam allowances toward the TAN BERRY PRINT square.

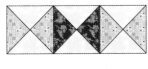

Make 30

4. Referring to the block illustration, sew Step 2 triangle blocks to both sides of the remaining Step 1 triangle blocks. Press the seam allowances toward the Step 2 triangle blocks. Sew these units to the top and bottom of the Step 3 units; press. <u>At this point each star block should measure 9-1/2 inches square.</u>

Make 30

Quilt Center

Cutting

From MEDIUM GREEN PRINT cut
- 36—1-1/2 x 42-inch strips.

From TAN BERRY PRINT cut
- 18—1-1/2 x 42-inch strips.

From GREEN PRINT cut
- 4—3-1/2 x 42-inch strips; from the strips cut 42—3-1/2-inch square lattice posts.

Quilt Center Assembly

1. Aligning long edges, sew a 1-1/2-inch wide MEDIUM GREEN PRINT strip to both sides of a 1-1/2-inch wide TAN BERRY PRINT strip. Refer to page 220 for **Hints and Helps for Pressing Strip Sets**. Make 18 strip sets. Cut the strip sets into pieced lattice segments.

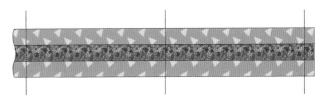

Crosscut 71, 9-1/2-inch long pieced lattice segments

2. Referring to the quilt illustration, sew together 6 of the 9-1/2-inch long pieced lattice segments and 5 of the star blocks. Press the seam allowances toward the lattice segments. Make 6 block rows. <u>At this point each block row should measure 9-1/2 x 63-1/2 inches.</u>

3. Referring to the quilt diagram, sew together 5 of the 9-1/2-inch long pieced lattice segments and 6 of the 3-1/2-inch square GREEN PRINT lattice posts. Press the seam allowances toward the lattice segments. Make 7 lattice strips. <u>At this point each lattice strip should measure 3-1/2 x 63-1/2 inches.</u>

4. Pin the block rows and lattice strips together at the block intersections and sew. Press the seam allowances in one direction. <u>At this point the quilt center should measure 63-1/2 x 75-1/2 inches.</u>

Border

Refer to **Binding and Diagonal Piecing** on page 221 for complete instructions with detailed illustrations.

NOTE: The yardage given allows for the border strips to be cut on the crosswise grain.

Cutting

From **RED PRINT** cut
- 10—9-1/2 x 42-inch border strips.

Attaching the Border

1. Measure the quilt from left to right through the center to determine the length of the top and bottom border strips. Cut 2, 9-1/2-inch wide RED PRINT strips to this measurement and pin them to the top and bottom of the quilt. Sew the strips to the quilt and press the seam allowances toward the border.

2. Measure the quilt from the top to bottom through the center, including the border strips just added, to determine the length of the side border strips. Cut 2, 9-1/2-inch wide RED PRINT strips to this measurement and pin them to the sides of the quilt. Sew the strips to the quilt and press the seam allowances toward the border.

Putting It All Together

Cut the 7-1/8 yard length of backing fabric in thirds crosswise to make 3, 2-3/8-yard lengths.

Refer to **Finishing the Quilt** on page 221 for complete instructions.

Binding the Quilt

Refer to **Binding and Diagonal Piecing** on page 221 for complete instructions with detailed illustrations.

NOTE: The 2-3/4-inch strips will produce a 1/2-inch wide finished double binding. If you would like a wider or narrower binding, adjust the width of the strips.

Cutting

From **GREEN PRINT** cut
- 10—2-3/4 x 42-inch strips.

Sew the binding to the quilt using a 3/8-inch seam allowance.

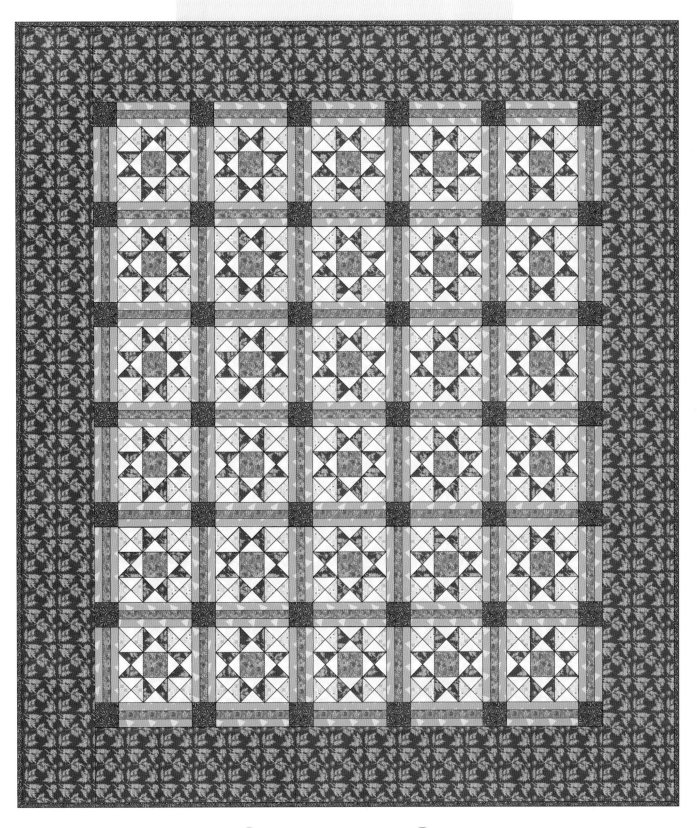

September Stars

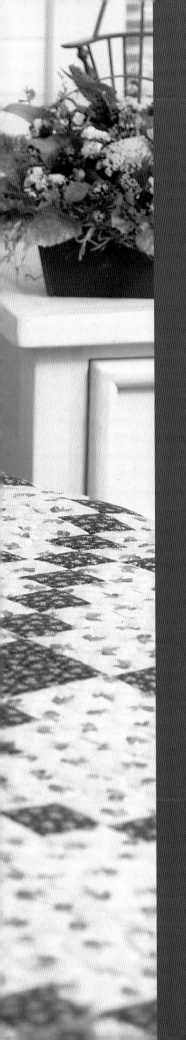

Sunny Side Up

For this variation of the traditional Irish Chain, a variety of small, medium and large prints contribute to the bed quilt's relaxing look and feel. Mixed with antique quilts and vintage pillows, it brings back fond memories of tranquil days and restful nights.

Sunny Side Up

Quilt measures 72 x 90 inches.
Block measures 16 inches square.

Fabric & Supplies

1-7/8 yards	**BLUE PRINT #1** for blocks, lattice posts, and middle border
2-2/3 yards	**BEIGE PRINT** for blocks and lattice
2-3/4 yards	**LARGE BLUE FLORAL** for blocks and outer border
2/3 yard	**GREEN PRINT** for inner border
7/8 yard	**BLUE PRINT #2** for binding
5-1/4 yards	Backing fabric
Quilt batting	76 x 94 inches

NOTE: read **Getting Started**, page 216, before beginning this project.

Blocks

Make 12 Blocks

Cutting

From **BLUE PRINT #1** cut
- 12—2-1/2 x 42-inch strips; from one of the strips cut
  1—2-1/2 x 12-inch strip.
- 2—4-1/2 x 42-inch strips; from the strips cut
  12—4-1/2-inch squares.

From **BEIGE PRINT** cut
- 5—4-1/2 x 42-inch strips.
- 6—4-1/2 x 42-inch strips; from the strips cut
  34—4-1/2 x 6-1/2-inch rectangles.
- 6—2-1/2 x 42-inch strips.

From **LARGE BLUE FLORAL** cut
- 2—4-1/2 x 42-inch strips.
- 3—4-1/2 x 42-inch strips; from the strips cut
  14—4-1/2 x 6-1/2-inch rectangles.
- 3—2-1/2 x 42-inch strips; from one of the strips cut
  2—2-1/2 x 12-inch strips.

NOTE: *The blocks are made up of strip sets. Refer to* **Hints and Helps for Pressing Strip Sets** *on page 220.*

Piecing

1. Aligning long edges, sew together a 2-1/2 x 42-inch BLUE PRINT #1 strip and a 4-1/2 x 42-inch BEIGE PRINT strip; press. Make 5 strip sets. Cut the strip sets into segments.

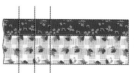

Strip Set A

Crosscut 68, 2-1/2-inch wide segments

2. Aligning long edges, sew 2-1/2 x 42-inch BEIGE PRINT strips to both sides of a 2-1/2 x 42-inch BLUE PRINT #1 strip; press. Make 2 strip sets. Cut the strip sets into segments.

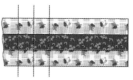

Strip Set B

Crosscut 24, 2-1/2-inch wide segments

3. Aligning long edges, sew a 2-1/2 x 42-inch LARGE BLUE FLORAL strip to a 2-1/2 x 42-inch BLUE PRINT #1 strip; press. Add a 2-1/2 x 42-inch BEIGE PRINT strip to the opposite side of the BLUE PRINT #1 strip; press. Make 2 strip sets. Cut the strip sets into segments.

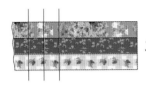

Strip Set C

Crosscut 20, 2-1/2-inch wide segments

4. Aligning long edges, sew 2-1/2 x 12-inch LARGE BLUE FLORAL strips to both sides of the 2-1/2 x 12-inch BLUE PRINT #1 strip; press. Make 1 strip set. Cut the strip set into segments.

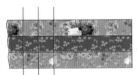

Strip Set D

Crosscut 4, 2-1/2-inch wide segments

5. Aligning long edges, sew together a 2-1/2 x 42-inch BLUE PRINT #1 strip and a 4-1/2 x 42-inch LARGE BLUE FLORAL strip; press. Make 2 strip sets. Cut the strip sets into segments.

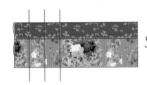

Strip Set E

Crosscut 28, 2-1/2-inch wide segments

6. To make Unit 1, sew Strip Set A segments to both sides of a Strip Set B segment; press. At this point each unit should measure 6-1/2 inches square.

Unit 1

Make 24

7. To make Unit II, sew a Strip Set A segment to one side of a Strip Set C segment; press. Sew a Strip Set E segment to the opposite side of the Strip Set C segment; press. At this point each unit should measure 6-1/2 inches square.

Unit II

Make 20

8. To make Unit III, sew Strip Set E segments to both sides of a Strip Set D segment; press. At this point each unit should measure 6-1/2 inches square.

Unit III

Make 4

9. To make Block A, sew a Unit 1 to both sides of a 4-1/2 x 6-1/2-inch BEIGE PRINT rectangle; press. Make 2 sections. Sew a 4-1/2 x 6-1/2-inch BEIGE PRINT rectangle to both sides of a 4-1/2-inch BLUE PRINT # 1 square; press. Referring to the block illustration, sew the 3 sections together; press. At this point each block should measure 16-1/2 inches square.

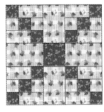

Block A

Make 2

10. To make Block B, sew a Unit II to both sides of a 4-1/2 x 6-1/2-inch LARGE BLUE FLORAL rectangle; press. Sew a 4-1/2 x 6-1/2-inch BEIGE PRINT rectangle to both sides of a 4-1/2-inch BLUE PRINT #1 square; press. Sew a Unit 1 to both sides of a 4-1/2 x 6-1/2-inch BEIGE PRINT rectangle; press. Referring to the block diagram, sew the 3 sections together; press. At this point each block should measure 16-1/2 inches square.

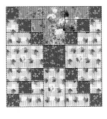

Block B

Make 6

11. To make Block C, sew a Unit III to one side of a 4-1/2 x 6-1/2-inch LARGE BLUE FLORAL rectangle; press. Sew a Unit II to the opposite side of the rectangle; press. Sew a 4-1/2 x 6-1/2-inch LARGE BLUE FLORAL rectangle to one side of a 4-1/2-inch BLUE PRINT #1 square. Sew a 4-1/2 x 6-1/2-inch BEIGE PRINT rectangle to the opposite side of the BLUE PRINT #1 square; press. Sew a Unit II to one side of a 4-1/2 x 6-1/2-inch BEIGE PRINT rectangle; press. Sew a Unit I to the opposite side of the rectangle; press. Referring to the block illustration, sew the 3 sections together; press. <u>At this point each block should measure 16-1/2-inches square.</u>

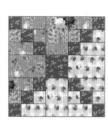

Block C

Make 4

Quilt Center

Cutting

From **BEIGE PRINT** cut
- 9—2-1/2 x 42-inch strips; from the strips cut 17—2-1/2 x 16-1/2-inch lattice strips.

From **BLUE PRINT #1** cut
- 1—2-1/2 x 42-inch strip; from the strip cut 6—2-1/2-inch square lattice posts.

Quilt Center Assembly

1. To make the first block row, sew together 2, C Blocks, 1, B Block, and 2, 2-1/2 x 16-1/2-inch BEIGE PRINT lattice strips. Press the seam allowances toward the lattice strips. Repeat this process for the fourth block row.

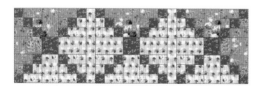

Make 2 block rows

2. To make the second block row, sew together 2, B Blocks, 1, A Block, and 2, 2-1/2 x 16-1/2-inch BEIGE PRINT lattice strips. Press the seam

allowances toward the lattice strips. Repeat this process for the third block row.

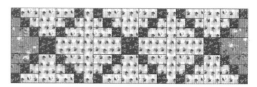

Make 2 block rows

3. Sew together 3, 2-1/2 x 16-1/2-inch BEIGE PRINT lattice strips and 2, 2-1/2-inch BLUE PRINT #1 lattice posts. Press the seam allowances toward the BEIGE PRINT strips. <u>At this point each lattice strip should measure 2-1/2 x 52-1/2 inches.</u>

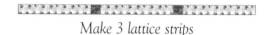

Make 3 lattice strips

4. Referring to the quilt illustration, sew together the block rows and the lattice strips to form the quilt center; press.

Borders

Refer to **Binding and Diagonal Piecing** on page 221 for complete instructions with detailed illustrations.

NOTE: The yardage given allows for the border strips to be cut on the crosswise grain.

Cutting

From **GREEN PRINT** cut
- 7—2-1/2 x 42-inch inner border strips.

From **BLUE PRINT #1** cut
- 8—2-1/2 x 42-inch middle border strips.

From **LARGE BLUE FLORAL** cut
- 9—6-1/2 x 42-inch outer border strips.

Attaching the Borders

1. Measure the quilt from left to right through the center to determine the length of the top and bottom inner border strips. Cut 2, 2-1/2-inch wide GREEN PRINT strips to this measurement and pin them to the top and bottom of the quilt. Sew the strips to the quilt and press the seam allowances toward the border.

2. Measure the quilt from the top to bottom through the center, including the border strips just added, to determine the length of the side inner border strips. Cut 2, 2-1/2-inch wide GREEN PRINT strips to this measurement and pin them to the sides of the quilt. Sew the strips to the quilt and press the seam allowances toward the border.

3. Measure the quilt from left to right through the center to determine the length of the top and bottom middle border strips. Cut 2, 2-1/2-inch wide BLUE PRINT #1 strips to this measurement and pin them to the top and bottom of the quilt. Sew the strips to the quilt and press the seam allowances toward the border.

4. Measure the quilt from the top to bottom through the center, including the border strips just added, to determine the length of the side middle border strips. Cut 2, 2-1/2-inch wide BLUE PRINT #1 strips to this measurement and pin them to the sides of the quilt. Sew the strips to the quilt and press the seam allowances toward the border.

5. Measure the quilt from left to right through the center to determine the length of the top and bottom outer border strips. Cut 2, 6-1/2-inch wide LARGE BLUE FLORAL strips to this measurement and pin them to the top and bottom of the quilt. Sew the strips to the quilt and press the seam allowances toward the border.

6. Measure the quilt from top to bottom through the center, including the border strips just added to determine the length of the side outer border strips. Cut 2, 6-1/2-inch wide LARGE BLUE FLORAL strips to this measurement and pin them to the sides of the quilt. Sew the strips to the quilt and press the seam allowances toward the border.

Putting It All Together

Cut the 5-1/4 yard length of backing fabric in half crosswise to make 2, 2-5/8-yard lengths.

Refer to **Finishing the Quilt** on page 221 for complete instructions.

Binding the Quilt

Refer to **Binding and Diagonal Piecing** on page 221 for complete instructions with detailed illustrations.

NOTE: *The 2-3/4-inch strips will produce a 1/2-inch wide finished double binding. If you would like a wider or narrower binding, adjust the width of the strips.*

Cutting

From **BLUE PRINT #2** cut
• 9—2-3/4 x 42-inch strips.

Sew the binding to the quilt using a 3/8-inch seam allowance.

Sunny Side Up

213

RESOURCES

Helpful Hints

Quilting is an art, not a science. However, to make the best use of your time and materials, it is important to be familiar with the tried and true method that Lynette Jensen has developed for easy cutting, piecing, appliqué, and quilting.

Begin by reading the General Instructions thoroughly. When you've finished, choose a quilt that suits your style and need (for reference, a small photo of each quilt accompanies its listing in the Project Index).

Save the Quilting Guides for last. When you've completed your quilting project, you'll have a better idea of what you'll want to add for the finishing touches.

But most of all, throughout the creative and soul-satisfying process of quilting—enjoy!

My Grabbit magnetic pin cushion has a surface that is large enough to hold lots of straight pins and a strong magnet that keeps them securely in place.

Silk pins are long and thin, which means they won't leave large holes in your fabric. I like them because they increase accuracy in pinning pieces or blocks together and it is easy to press over silk pins as well.

For pressing individual pieces, blocks, and quilt tops, I use an 18 x 48-inch sheet of plywood covered with several layers of cotton fiberfill and topped with a layer of muslin stapled to the back. The 48-inch length allows me to press an entire width of fabric at one time without the need to reposition it, and the square ends are better than tapered ends on an ironing board for pressing finished quilt tops.

Rotary Cutting

SAFETY FIRST! The blades of a rotary cutter are very sharp and need to be for accurate cutting. Look at a variety of cutters to find one that feels good in your hand. All quality cutters have a safety mechanism to "close" the cutting blade when not in use. After each cut and before laying the rotary cutter down, close the blade. Soon this will become second nature to you and will prevent dangerous accidents. Always keep cutters out of the sight of children. Rotary cutters are very tempting to fiddle with when they are lying around. When your blade is dull or nicked, change it. Damaged blades do not cut accurately and require extra effort that can also result in slipping and injury. Also, always cut away from yourself for safety.

Fold the fabric in half lengthwise matching the selvage edges.

"Square off" the ends of your fabric before measuring and cutting pieces. This means that the cut edge of the fabric must be exactly perpendicular to the folded edge which creates a 90° angle. Align the folded and selvage edges of the fabric with the lines on the

6 x 24" ruler

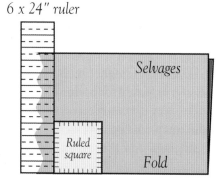

cutting board, and place a ruled square on the fold. Place a 6 x 24-inch ruler against the side of the square to get a 90° angle. Hold the ruler in place, remove the square, and cut along the edge of the ruler. If you are left-handed, work from the other end of the fabric. Use the lines on your cutting board to help line up fabric, but not to measure and cut strips. Use a ruler for accurate cutting, always checking to make sure your fabric is lined up with horizontal and vertical lines on the ruler.

Cutting Strips

When cutting strips or rectangles, cut on the crosswise grain. Strips can then be cut into squares or smaller rectangles.

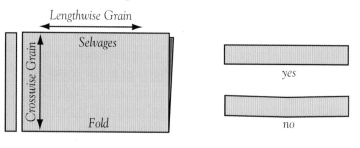

If your strips are not straight after cutting a few of them, refold the fabric, align the folded and selvage edges with the lines on the cutting board, and "square off" the edge again by trimming to straighten, and begin cutting.

Trimming Side and Corner Triangles

In projects with side and corner triangles, the instructions have you cut side and corner triangles larger than needed. This will allow you to square up the quilt and eliminates the frustration of ending up with precut side and corner triangles that don't match the size of your pieced blocks.

To cut triangles, first cut squares. The project directions will tell you what size to make the squares and whether to cut them in half to make two triangles

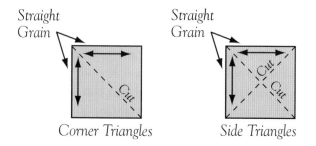

Corner Triangles   Side Triangles

or to cut them in quarters to make four triangles, as shown in the diagrams. This cutting method will give you side triangles that have the straight grain on the outside edges of the quilt. This is a very important part of quilt-making that will help stabilize your quilt center.

Helpful Hints for Sewing with Flannel

Always prewash and machine dry flannel. This will prevent severe shrinkage after the quilt is made. Some flannels shrink more than others. For this reason, we have allowed approximately 1/4 yard extra for each fabric under the fabric requirements. Treat the more heavily napped side of solid flannels as the right side of the fabric.

Because flannel stretches more than other cotton calicos and because the nap makes them thicker, the quilt design should be simple. Let the fabric and color make the design statement.

Consider combining regular cotton calicos with flannels. The different textures complement each other nicely.

Use a 10 to 12 stitches per inch setting on your machine. A 1/4-inch seam allowance is also recommended for flannel piecing.

When sewing triangle-pieced squares together, take extra care not to stretch the diagonal seam. Trim off the points from the seam allowances to eliminate bulk.

Press gently to prevent stretching pieces out of shape.

Check block measurements as you progress. "Square up" the blocks as needed. Flannel will shift and it is easy to end up with blocks that are misshapen. If you trim and measure as you go, you are more likely to have accurate blocks. If you notice a piece of flannel is stretching more than the others, place it on the bottom when stitching on the machine. The natural action of the feed dogs will help prevent it from stretching.

Before stitching pieces, strips, or borders together, pin often to prevent fabric from stretching and moving. When stitching longer pieces together, divide the pieces into quarters and pin. Divide into even smaller sections to get more control.

Use a lightweight batting to prevent the quilt from becoming too heavy.

Cutting Triangles from Squares

Cutting accurate triangles can be intimidating for beginners, but a clear plastic ruler, rotary cutter, and cutting mat are all that are needed to make perfect triangles. The cutting instructions often direct you to cut strips, then squares, and then triangles.

Sewing Layered Strips Together

When you are instructed to layer strips, right sides together, and sew, you need to take some precautions. Gently lay a strip on top of another, carefully lining up the raw edges. Pressing the strips together will hold them together nicely, and a few pins here and there will also help. Be careful not to stretch the strips as you sew them together.

Rod Casing or Sleeve to Hang Quilts

To hang wall quilts, attach a casing that is made of the same fabric as the quilt back. Attach this casing at the top of the quilt, just below the binding. Often, it is helpful to attach a second casing at the bottom of the quilt so you can insert a dowel into it which will help weight the quilt and make it hang free of ripples.

To make a rod casing or "sleeve," cut enough strips of fabric equal to the width of the quilt plus 2 inches for side hems. Generally, 6-inch wide strips will accommodate most rods. If you are using a rod with a larger diameter, increase the width of the strips.

Seam the strips together to get the length needed; press. Fold the strip in half lengthwise, wrong sides together. Stitch the long raw edges together with a 1/4-inch seam allowance. Center the seam on the backside of the sleeve; press. The raw edges of the seam will be concealed when the sleeve is stitched to the back of the quilt. Turn under both of the short raw edges; press and stitch to hem the ends. The final measurement should be about 1/2 inch from the quilt edges.

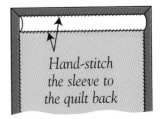

Hand-stitch the sleeve to the quilt back

Pin the sleeve to the back of the quilt so the top edge of the sleeve is just below the binding. Hand-stitch the top edge of the sleeve in place, then the bottom edge. Make sure to knot and secure your stitches at each end of the sleeve to make sure it will not pull away from the quilt with use. Slip the rod into the casing. If your wall quilt is not directional, making a sleeve for the bottom edge will allow you to turn your quilt end to end to relieve the stress at the top edge. You could also slip a dowel into the bottom sleeve to help anchor the lower edge of the wall quilt.

Choosing a Quilt Design

Quilting is such an individual process that it is difficult to recommend designs for each quilt. There are hundreds of quilting stencils available at quilt shops. (Templates are used generally for appliqué shapes; stencils are used for marking quilting designs.)

There are a few suggestions that may help you decide how to quilt your project, depending on how much time you would like to spend quilting. Many quilters now use professional long-arm quilting machines or hire someone skilled at running these machines to do the quilting. This, of course, frees up more time to piece.

Quilting Suggestions

Repeat one of the design elements in the quilt as part of the quilting design.

Two or three parallel rows of echo quilting outside an appliqué piece will highlight the shape.

Stipple or meander quilting behind a feather or central motif will make the primary design more prominent.

Look for quilting designs that will cover two or more borders, rather than choosing separate designs for each individual border.

Quilting in the ditch of seams is an effective way to get a project quilted without a great deal of time marking the quilt.

Marking the Quilting Design

When marking the quilt top, use a marking tool that will be visible on the quilt fabric and yet will be easy enough to remove. Always test your marking tool on a scrap of fabric before marking the entire quilt.

Along with a multitude of commercial marking tools available, you may find that very thin slivers of hand soap (Dial, Ivory, etc.) work really well for marking medium to dark color fabrics. The thin lines of soap show up nicely and they are easily removed by simply rubbing gently with a piece of like-colored fabric.

Hints and Helps for Pressing Strip Sets

Avoid this rainbow effect

When sewing strips of fabric together for strip sets, it is important to press the seam allowances nice and flat, usually to the darker fabric. Be careful not to stretch as you press, causing a "rainbow effect." This will affect the accuracy and shape of the pieces cut from the strip set. I like to press on the wrong side first and with the strips perpendicular to the ironing board. Then I flip the piece over and press on the right side to prevent little pleats from forming at the seams. Laying the strip set lengthwise on the ironing board seems to encourage the rainbow effect, as shown in the diagram.

Borders

NOTE: *Cut borders to the width called for. Always cut border strips a few inches longer than needed, just to be safe. Diagonally piece the border strips together as needed.*

1. With pins, mark the center points along all 4 sides of the quilt. For the top and bottom borders, measure the quilt from left to right through the middle.

2. Measure and mark the border lengths and center points on the strips cut for the borders before sewing them on.

3. Pin the border strips to the quilt and stitch a 1/4-inch seam. Press the seam allowances toward the border. Trim off excess border lengths.

Trim away excess fabric

4. For the side borders, measure your quilt from top to bottom, including the borders just added, to determine the length of the side borders.

5. Measure and mark the side border lengths as you did for the top and bottom borders.

6. Pin and stitch the side border strips in place. Press and trim the border strips even with the borders just added.

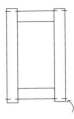

Trim away excess fabric

7. If your quilt has multiple borders, measure, mark, and sew additional borders to the quilt in the same manner.

Decorative Stitches

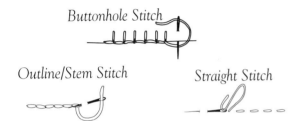

Buttonhole Stitch

Outline/Stem Stitch

Straight Stitch

Finishing the Quilt

1. Remove the selvages from the backing fabric. Sew the long edges together, and press. Trim the backing and batting so they are 2 inches to 4 inches larger than the quilt top.

2. Mark the quilt top for quilting. Layer the backing, batting, and quilt top. Baste the 3 layers together and quilt.

3. When quilting is complete, remove basting. Hand-baste all 3 layers together a scant 1/4 inch from the edge. This hand-basting keeps the layers from shifting and prevents puckers from forming when adding the binding. Trim excess batting and backing fabric even with the edge of the quilt top. Add the binding as shown below.

Binding and Diagonal Piecing

Diagonal Piecing

Stitch diagonally

Trim to 1/4-inch seam allowance

Press seam open

1. Diagonally piece the binding strips. Fold the strip in half lengthwise, wrong sides together, and press.

Double-layer Binding

2. Unfold and trim one end at a 45° angle. Turn under the edge 1/4 inch and press. Refold the strip.

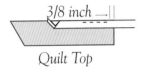

Fold line

3. With raw edges of the binding and quilt top even, stitch with a 3/8-inch seam allowance, starting 2 inches from the angled end.

4. Miter the binding at the corners. As you approach a corner of the quilt, stop sewing 3/8 inch from the corner of the quilt.

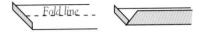

3/8 inch

Quilt Top

5. Clip the threads and remove the quilt from under the presser foot. Flip the binding strip up and away from the quilt, then fold the binding down even with the raw edge of the quilt. Begin sewing at the upper edge. Miter all 4 corners in this manner.

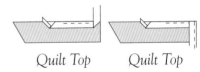

Quilt Top   *Quilt Top*

6. Trim the end of the binding so it can be tucked inside of the beginning binding about 3/8 inch. Finish stitching the seam.

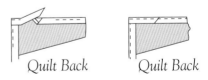

Quilt Back   *Quilt Back*

7. Turn the folded edge of the binding over the raw edges and to the back of the quilt so that the stitching line does not show. Hand-sew the binding in place, folding in the mitered corners as you stitch.

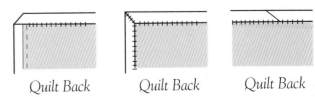

Quilt Back   *Quilt Back*   *Quilt Back*

Depending on the size and detail

of your quilt pattern, refer to the quilting guides Lynette selected for several of the quilts featured in this book, or quilt as desired using commercial quilt stencils.

Holiday Bouquet

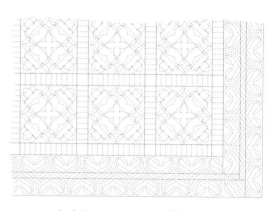

Harvest Patches

Stone Creek

Sunporch Basket

Daisy Days Nine-Patch

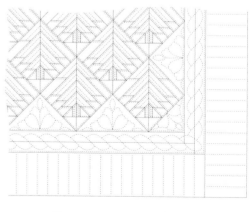

Prairie Pines

Quilting GUIDES

Courtyard Garden

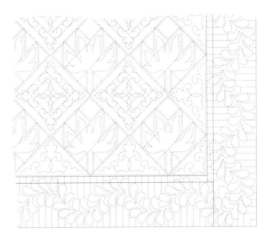

Cabin Maples

Crossroads

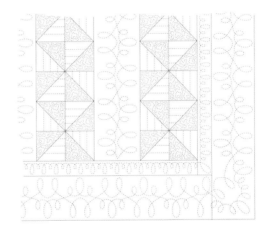

Party Pinwheels

September Stars

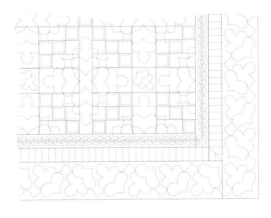

Sunny Side Up

THIMBLEBERRIES®